Key Stage Three

Shakespeare

Richard III

This book is for 11-14 year olds.

It's packed with all the really important stuff you need to know about *Richard III* if you want to do well in your Key Stage Three SAT Shakespeare Question.

We've stuck loads of pictures and jokes in to make it more fun — so you'll actually use it.

Simple as that.

Contents

SECTION 5 — WRITING AN ESSAY

SECTION 6 — TYPES OF QUESTION

SECTION 7 — THE SET SCENES

Published by Coordination Group Publications Ltd.

Contributors:
Katherine Reed
Edward Robinson
Elisabeth Sanderson
Gerry Spatharis
Nicola Woodfin

With thanks to Keri Barrow and Paula Barnett for the proofreading.

ISBN   1 84146 369 8

Groovy website: www.cgpbooks.co.uk

Jolly bits of clipart from CorelDRAW

Printed by Elanders Hindson, Newcastle upon Tyne.

Preparing Your Answer

<u>Preparation</u> is the key to doing well in your <u>exam</u>. So, before you start writing, <u>plan</u> what you're going to write. This will make everything <u>a lot easier</u>, even if it sounds like loads of extra work.

You Have to Know the *Set Scenes* Really Well

1) The Shakespeare paper tests how well you <u>know the play</u>.
2) It's all about the <u>set scenes</u>. Your teacher will tell you which the set scenes are — if you ask them nicely...
3) You have to know these scenes <u>like the back of your hand</u>.

Learn your set scenes... or the puppy gets it.

You'll <u>know</u> which bits of the play you have to write about <u>before the exam</u> — which means you won't get any <u>nasty surprises</u> on the day. As long as you've learnt 'em, that is.

Take Time to *Plan* Your Answers

Planning might seem like a waste of precious exam time. But if you just start writing without planning you'll end up <u>spouting rubbish</u>. Planning makes your answer <u>loads better</u>.

1) <u>Read</u> the question. <u>Check it out</u> carefully. It could be <u>two questions squished into one</u>:

> **e.g.** Q. In Act 1, Scene 2, what is Anne's opinion of Richard and how does Richard try to change this opinion?

What is Anne's opinion of Richard?   How does Richard try to change this opinion?

2) <u>Read through the scenes again</u>. Look for <u>anything the characters say</u> that will <u>help</u> you answer the question. When you find something useful, <u>underline</u> it. E.g. For the first part of the question above you would look for <u>anything</u> that Anne says about <u>Richard</u>.

3) Next, think about what the <u>main points</u> of your essay will be. Make a list.

Do you see my point?

> **e.g.**
> • what Anne thinks about Richard
> • the reasons she feels like this
> • how Richard tries to win his way into Anne's affections
> • Anne's initial response to Richard's attempts to win her over
> • how she feels about him by the end of the scene

4) Include <u>all your main points</u> in the essay. Then you'll be on your way to a <u>good mark</u>.

Preparation, that's what you need...

You'll feel a lot more <u>relaxed</u> once you've got a good <u>plan</u> to fall back on. Once that's sorted you can <u>focus</u> on each point <u>one at a time</u>. This makes the whole exam thing a lot <u>less scary</u>.

Writing Well and Giving Examples

Examiners are a funny lot, but it's easy enough to impress them if you know what makes them tick. Here's a few useful little tricks that'll have them gasping in admiration.

Use Examples to Show You Know Your Stuff

It's crucial that you use examples. They show evidence of the points you're making. As my old granny used to say, "An opinion without an example is like a boy-band without a rubbish dance routine." Or something.

Quotes are really useful examples. Examiners love 'em. Remember to:

I couldn't unlock the key scenes.

1) Start and end quotes with speech marks.
2) Copy out the words exactly as they are in the play.
3) Explain why the quote is a good example — what does it tell you?

Sort Out Your Writing

1) Sound enthusiastic about the play. Use plenty of adjectives (descriptive words).

e.g. *The atmosphere in this scene is very tense and menacing — Shakespeare shows the audience that Richard is an evil character who will stop at nothing in order to become King.*

2) Check your spelling and punctuation. Otherwise the examiner might not know what you mean.

3) Write in paragraphs. A page that's full of writing with no breaks is tough to read. Remember, a new topic = a new paragraph.

Write About Versions of the Play You've Seen

If you've seen a film or theatre version of the play, you can write about that too — as long as it relates to the question.

This is another good way of sounding interested in the play. Just make sure you mention which version of the play you saw.

Keep in mind that each version can be very different. The costumes, settings and personalities of the characters can all vary.

e.g. *In the production of the play I saw in Barnsley in 2002, the director, Ivor Megaphone, brought out the sense of danger in this scene by reducing the lighting and making Richard talk in a quiet, calculating way.*

I'll make an exam-ple of you...

Exams aren't really that complicated. They ask you a question, you answer it. If you're prepared, there'll be no nasty surprises. Stick to the point, and there's nowt to worry about.

Stage Directions, Acts and Scenes

It's really important you know what <u>stage directions</u>, <u>acts</u> and <u>scenes</u> are. Acts and scenes are like the <u>skeleton</u> of the play, and stage directions tell you what's going on <u>on-stage</u>.

Stage Directions *Tell You Who's Doing What*

<u>Stage directions</u> tell the actors what to do, e.g. <u>when to come on stage</u> and <u>when to go off</u>. They sometimes say <u>who</u> they have to talk to as well. They're usually written in <u>italics</u> or put in <u>brackets</u>:

The <u>names</u> of the characters are written here to tell you who's <u>speaking</u>.

This stage direction means Catesby <u>walks onto the stage</u>.

[Enter Catesby]

CATESBY Madam, his majesty doth call for you,
    And for your grace, and you, my gracious lord.
ELIZABETH Catesby, I come. Lords, will you go with me?
RIVERS We wait upon your grace.

[Exeunt all but Richard]

Act 1, Scene 3, 319-322

<u>Exeunt</u> means more than one person <u>leaves</u> the stage. So here, everyone except Richard walks off.

Which way to the station please?

The <u>line numbers</u> often <u>vary</u> in different printed versions of the play — so <u>don't worry</u> if these line numbers don't exactly match your copy.

Remember, plays are supposed to be <u>performed</u>, not read. So <u>stage directions</u> are really helpful for imagining how the play would look <u>on-stage</u>.

Acts <u>and</u> Scenes *Split Up the Play*

1) The play is divided up into <u>five</u> big chunks called <u>acts</u>. Each act tells us <u>part</u> of the story. Put them all together and you get the <u>whole</u> story.

2) Acts are also divided up into even <u>smaller</u> chunks called <u>scenes</u>. Scenes <u>break up</u> the story. A <u>new scene</u> might be in a <u>different place</u>, at a <u>different time</u>, or with <u>different characters</u>.

    E.g. If one scene is set in the <u>Tower</u>, the next scene could be <u>outside</u>, in a street. Or one scene might be set during the <u>day</u>, and the next at <u>night</u>.

Are you sure this is the right scene?

Stop it, you're making a scene...

<u>Acts</u> and <u>scenes</u> are actually <u>really handy</u>, as they can help you <u>find</u> the speech or bit of action you're looking for. Remember — the play has <u>5 acts</u> and <u>loads of scenes</u>.

Richard III as a Play

Check out these tips and you'll really get to grips with the play.

It's a Play, Not a Novel

It's meant to be acted, not just read. When you read the play, it's hard to imagine what it will look like on stage. Try and see the characters in your mind. Think about:

- what kind of people they are
- how you think they would say their lines
- how they would act

If you want some idea of how the play might look when it's acted out, you could watch it on video or DVD. Your school might have a copy of it — it's worth asking. Just remember: each version will be different.

Sometimes Characters Talk to Themselves

1) In real life, this is odd. In plays, it's normal — it doesn't mean they've gone bananas.

2) The characters talk to themselves to let the audience know what they are thinking and how they are feeling.

3) When someone talks to themself on an empty stage, it's called a soliloquy (or monologue).

4) If someone talks to the audience when there are other people on stage, it'll say [Aside] by their name in the play. The audience can hear what is being said, but the other characters can't.

Richard III is a History Play

Shakespeare wrote a series of plays about the history of the English Royal Family. Richard III follows on from Henry VI Part 3, and it's set about 80 years before Shakespeare was born.

Even though it's a history play, that doesn't mean it's pure fact. Shakespeare chose to base the play on the idea that Richard was a deformed murderer and Richmond was a good man — but this is only one of several versions of events. Shakespeare even made up some characters and changed some of the dates to make the play more entertaining for his audience.

Richard III is also sometimes called a tragedy, as the main character rises to power before losing and being killed, and there are loads of deaths.

Richard the Furred — Shakespeare acted by cats...

If you're not used to reading plays, it's bound to feel odd at first. The fact that the play was written ages ago, combined with the main characters being royals and nobles, takes some getting used to.

Odd Language

Some of this old language is hard to get your head round. But once you get the hang of reading it things will become a lot clearer. Just remember these rules:

Don't Stop Reading at the End of a Line

1) Follow the punctuation — read to the end of the sentence, not the end of the line.

e.g.
> All comfort that the dark night can afford
> Be to thy person, noble father-in-law.
>
> Act 5, Scene 3, 81-82

There's no full stop here so carry on to the next line.

2) These two lines actually make up one sentence:

> All comfort that the dark night can afford be to thy person, noble father-in-law.

3) Most lines start with a capital letter — but this doesn't always mean it's a new sentence.

4) Full stops, question marks and exclamation marks show you where the sentence ends.

Sometimes You Have to Switch the Words Around

1) Shakespeare likes to mess around with the order of words. It helps him fit the sentences into the poetry (see page 7).

2) If a piece of writing looks like it's back-to-front — don't panic.

e.g.
> Here in these confines slily have I lurked
>
> Act 4, Scene 4, line 3

3) Play around with the word order and it'll make sense. What this really says is:

> I have slily lurked here in these confines.

Sense make doesn't Shakespeare...

I know Shakespeare's language looks really different from the English we speak, but it's actually pretty similar. Once you've got the word order sorted you're well on the way to sussing it out.

More Odd Language

Shakespeare was around over <u>400 years ago</u> — so the language he uses can seem a bit <u>weird</u>. Some of the words are <u>old words</u> that we <u>don't use any more</u>.

Thou, Thee and Thy Come Up a Lot

Once you know what these words mean, things get <u>a lot easier</u>. Happy days.

Thou = you

Yet thou didst kill my children.
Act 4, Scene 4, 422

Thee = you

But now I tell thee — keep it to thyself —
Act 3, Scene 2, 102

Thy = your

O princely Buckingham, I'll kiss thy hand
Act 1, Scene 3, 279

Verbs Can Look Odd

Hast thou seen the size of this carrot?

Often, all that's different is there's a couple of <u>extra letters</u> on the end of the verb. Take off the <u>t</u> or <u>st</u> and you'll see what they mean.

 e.g.

hath, hast = has	wilt = will
didst = did	thinkst = think	speakst = speak

These verbs often go with <u>thou</u>, like this:

If thou wilt outstrip death, go cross the seas
Act 4, Scene 1, 41

Some Words are Squashed Together

The word <u>it</u> often gets <u>stuck to the next word</u>, and <u>loses the "i"</u>.

'Tis an outrage!

 e.g.

'twas = it was	'twere = it were
'tis = it is	is't = is it

An i for an i...

<u>Dropping letters</u> from words isn't that strange when you think about it. We still do it in modern English, like when we change <u>it is</u> to <u>it's</u>. Shakespeare just drops <u>different letters</u>.

Poetry

There's lots of <u>poetry</u> in Shakespeare's plays. If you understand the poetry, it'll <u>help you understand</u> some of the reasons behind the <u>strange language</u>.

How to Spot Poetry

<u>Prose</u> means writing that <u>isn't poetry</u>.
There's a lot of <u>poetry</u> in Richard III — and <u>here's how to spot it</u>:

> ### Poetry has:
> 1) Capital letters at the start of each line
> 2) 10, 11 or 12 syllables in each line

A <u>syllable</u> is a unit of sound. The word <u>poetry</u> has 3 syllables – <u>po e try</u>.

Poetry Doesn't Have to Rhyme

1) Some poetry <u>rhymes</u>, some <u>doesn't</u>.

e.g.
> I died for hope ere I could lend thee aid.
> But cheer thy heart and be thou not dismayed.
> God and good angels fight on Richmond's side,
> And Richard falls in height of all his pride.
> *Act 5, Scene 3, 174-177*

Each line starts with a <u>capital letter</u>.

e.g.
> I will converse with iron-witted fools
> And unrespective boys. None are for me
> That look into me with considerate eyes.
> High-reaching Buckingham grows circumspect.
> *Act 4, Scene 2, 28-31*

This bit of poetry is in <u>rhyming couplets</u> — the first line rhymes with the second, and the third rhymes with the fourth.

This <u>doesn't rhyme</u> — but it's <u>still poetry</u>.

2) The language sometimes sounds <u>strange</u> because Shakespeare tries to get <u>each line</u> to contain the <u>right amount of syllables</u>.

3) Most of Richard III is written in poetry — although some of the <u>less posh</u> characters, like the murderers, sometimes talk in <u>prose</u> (speech that isn't poetry).

You did ask for three silly bulls?

Leann Rimes — with what?

Once you realise you're dealing with <u>poetry</u>, it becomes much easier to work out <u>what it means</u>. And the rules for <u>spotting it</u> are pretty simple — just remember that it doesn't have to rhyme.

Revision Summary

Right, let's see how much you know about Bill Shakespeare and his odd little ways. If you haven't read any of Shakespeare's stuff before, it's easy to be flummoxed by the way he writes. But trust me, the more you read, the easier it gets. If you get stuck on any of these questions, look back through the section to find the answers. Then have another go, without looking back.

1) What's the point of stage directions?

2) What does "exeunt" mean?

3) What's the play split up into?

   a) Chapters and verses   b) Nooks and crannies   c) Acts and scenes

4) A play is meant to be:

   a) ignored   b) burnt   c) performed

5) What is a soliloquy?

6) If it says "Aside" by a character's name, who can hear what they're saying?

   a) The other characters   b) The audience   c) Belgians

7) The events in Richard III are:
   a) pure fact   b) just one version of events   c) set in Bulgaria

8) "A new line of poetry means it's a new sentence." True or false?

9) If a piece of writing doesn't make sense, what should you do?

   a) Change the word order   b) Phone a friend   c) Cry

10) When was Shakespeare around?

   a) 400 years ago   b) 200 years ago   c) 65 million years ago

11) What do these words mean?

   a) Thou   b) Hath   c) Didst   d) 'Twas

12) What does each line of poetry start with?

13) How many syllables are there in a line of poetry?

14) Does all poetry rhyme?

Am I the only one struggling with the lingo?

Who's Who in the Play

There are <u>loads</u> of characters in this play. Here are some of the important ones.

Richard III — the main baddie

RICHARD

He's sometimes called the <u>Duke of Gloucester</u>. He's the most important character. He makes things happen — most of them <u>bad</u>.

Buckingham and Richard's supporters

BUCKINGHAM

CATESBY

RATCLIFFE

<u>Buckingham</u> gives Richard a lot of <u>help</u>, but then they fall out and Richard has him <u>killed</u>. Richard hires <u>Tyrrel</u> to kill the young Princes. <u>Brakenbury</u>'s in charge of the Tower. <u>Catesby</u> and <u>Ratcliffe</u> are more cronies.

Edward IV and Queen Elizabeth

ELIZABETH

EDWARD IV

Edward IV is Richard III's <u>brother</u>. Edward IV is <u>King</u> to start with but he soon <u>dies</u>. Queen Elizabeth is his wife.

The Young Princes, sons of Edward IV and Elizabeth

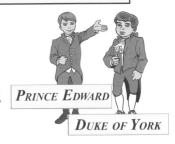

PRINCE EDWARD

DUKE OF YORK

Prince Edward is next in line to the <u>throne</u> after Edward IV dies. Richard has him and his brother, the young Duke of York, <u>killed</u>.

Clarence and Hastings

CLARENCE

HASTINGS

Clarence is Richard's other <u>brother</u>. Richard has him killed in Act 1. Hastings is a <u>nobleman</u> who is also killed by Richard.

Rivers, Dorset and Grey

GREY

RIVERS

These are the <u>Woodvilles</u>. Earl Rivers is <u>Queen Elizabeth's brother</u>. The Marquis of Dorset and Lord Grey are her <u>sons</u> by an earlier marriage. Richard has Rivers and Grey locked up and <u>executed</u>. Dorset gets away.

Queen Margaret, Lady Anne and The Duchess of York

<u>Queen Margaret</u> was married to <u>Henry VI</u>, the old King — until Richard killed him.

QUEEN MARGARET

LADY ANNE

DUCHESS OF YORK

<u>Lady Anne</u> was married to <u>Margaret's son</u>, until Richard killed him too. Richard marries Lady Anne then has her killed. The <u>Duchess</u> is Richard's mum.

Richmond and Stanley — Richard's opponents

RICHMOND

STANLEY

Richmond is Richard's <u>rival</u> for the throne. He <u>fights Richard</u> and kills him. Richmond becomes King Henry VII. Stanley is a nobleman who secretly <u>supports</u> Richmond.

Richard

As you might have guessed from the title, Richard is the <u>most important</u> character in the play.

He's <u>Ambitious</u> and <u>Determined</u> to Succeed

1) He's <u>bold</u> and <u>confident</u>. He tells us right at the start that he's out to <u>cause trouble</u>.

> I am determined to prove a villain
> Act 1, Scene 1, line 30

2) He's a good fighter and <u>brave in battle</u>.

3) He's very <u>ambitious</u>. He'll do <u>anything for power</u> — he's willing to have his own <u>brother</u> and his young <u>nephews</u> killed so that he can become <u>King</u>.

He's <u>Bad</u> Through and Through

1) Richard says he's so <u>ugly</u> that the dogs bark at him. He's "<u>deformed</u>" and lame. Some of the other characters comment on his bad looks too.

2) In Shakespeare's time, an audience would expect a character who <u>looked bad</u> to <u>behave badly</u> — and Richard doesn't disappoint them. He <u>chooses</u> to be bad.

3) Several <u>other characters</u> say they're <u>sorry</u> for their bad deeds before they die, but Richard <u>doesn't</u>.

> Conscience is but a word that cowards use
> Act 5, Scene 3, line 310

4) He only cares about himself. He's <u>two-faced</u> and <u>unreliable</u> — even to the people who help him. He <u>uses people</u> then gets rid of them.

He's <u>Crafty</u> and <u>Clever</u> — and a <u>Great Actor</u>

1) Richard can be <u>witty</u> and <u>charming</u> as well as <u>sarcastic</u>. He <u>flatters people</u> and fools them with his clever words. He sets out to persuade <u>Lady Anne</u> to marry him — even though he has just <u>killed her husband</u> — and he manages it.

2) He's good at <u>changing</u> the way he <u>speaks</u> to play different parts. When he woos Lady Anne he pretends to be <u>romantic</u>. He acts the <u>sympathetic brother</u> with Clarence and he's <u>humble</u> and <u>religious</u> in front of the Mayor and citizens. It's all just an <u>act</u>.

> You should hear my Johnny Vegas impression. Monkey!

3) He tells loads of <u>lies</u>, e.g. he spreads rumours about the young Princes being <u>illegitimate</u> so that he can be King. He promises Buckingham <u>rewards</u> for his help, but never delivers them.

You know I'm bad, I'm bad, I'm really really bad...

Richard is an out-and-out villain — we have absolutely no sympathy whatsoever when he cops it. But at the same time, you can't help admiring his cleverness and determination. Ooh, he's a devil...

Edward IV, Queen Elizabeth & The Young Princes

King Edward IV is married to Queen Elizabeth. They have two young sons — Edward, Prince of Wales and Richard, Duke of York. They have a daughter too, called Elizabeth, but she doesn't appear.

Edward IV Tries but Fails to Keep Peace

1) At the start, Edward IV is King. He's ill and dies early in the play.

2) Edward IV's suspicious of his brother Clarence. Richard persuades Edward to have Clarence killed. Edward changes his mind afterwards but can't save Clarence. He feels really guilty about Clarence's death.

3) Edward seems to be a decent King but his judgement is poor. He made a big mistake in trusting Richard.

4) Edward tries to make sure everyone has sorted out their quarrels before he dies. He insists they all make up and swear to be friends. He wants to die with a clear conscience.

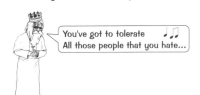

You've got to tolerate ♪♫
All those people that you hate...

And more in peace my soul shall part to heaven,
Since I have made my friends at peace on earth
Act 2, Scene 1, 5-6

Queen Elizabeth Survives

1) Queen Elizabeth's genuinely upset when her husband, Edward IV, dies. She says she could cry enough to "drown the world". After Edward's death, her brother, Rivers, and one of her sons, Grey, are executed. Later on her two youngest sons are killed by Richard.

2) Queen Elizabeth learns to stand up for herself as the play goes on. At first she's not very strong — she rushes off into sanctuary (safety in church) when Richard arrests Rivers and Grey. But by the end of the play she stands up to Richard. She interrupts him and argues when he asks to marry her daughter.

3) She's clever enough to protect her daughter, also called Elizabeth, from Richard and then arrange for her to marry Richmond instead.

The Young Princes are Innocent Victims

1) Prince Edward and his brother the Duke of York are only children, but they're next in line to the throne after Edward IV dies. They behave so well that it's shocking when they die. Even their murderer Tyrrel (see p.16) feels bad about them being killed.

But we're so cute...

2) Prince Edward is brave and obedient — even though he's anxious about staying in the Tower. He wants to serve his country well.

3) The Duke of York is witty and lively. He's almost as good at word play as his Uncle Richard.

Get out, before I have you throne out...

Richard plays his brother Edward IV like a trumpet — he gets him to do exactly what Richard wants. Elizabeth starts off a bit rubbish but in the end she double-crosses Richard, so fair play to her.

Lady Anne, Queen Margaret & The Duchess of York

These three women are quite <u>different</u> from each other — but they all <u>hate Richard</u>.

Lady Anne <u>is Another of</u> Richard's Victims

1) She was married to the old <u>Prince Edward</u>, but Richard <u>killed</u> him and his father, Henry VI. She <u>curses</u> Richard pretty viciously — she even calls him a "foul lump of deformity" — but Richard still persuades her to <u>marry him</u>.

2) Lady Anne's quite <u>weak</u> and <u>lonely</u>. She doesn't want to be Queen and she seems <u>unhappy</u> all the time.

> Well, no one's perfect. At least Richard's got prospects...

3) She is <u>kind</u> to Clarence's children and tries to visit the young Princes in the Tower. The Young <u>Duke of York</u> is very fond of her. The <u>Duchess of York</u> likes her too.

4) Richard <u>gets rid of Anne</u> very quickly after marrying her, because he decides he wants to marry Queen Elizabeth's daughter. He starts a rumour that Anne's <u>ill</u>. The next thing we hear is that she's <u>dead</u>.

Queen Margaret <u>Curses Everyone</u>

1) She's <u>bitter</u> and <u>angry</u> right from the start of the play. Her husband, Henry VI, and son were killed by Richard. She thinks she should <u>still be Queen</u> and she wants <u>revenge</u> for her dead husband and son.

2) She's ferocious and good with words. Some of her <u>curses</u> are great. She calls Richard a "bottled spider" and she <u>stands up to him</u> even when he makes fun of her.

3) The others <u>laugh</u> at Margaret at first. She predicts that they'll be sorry and she's <u>right</u>. She even <u>warns Buckingham</u> against Richard but he ignores her.

4) Later on, she <u>gloats</u> at all the destruction Richard has caused. She thinks it serves them all right.

The <u>Duchess of York</u> Hates her Son Richard

1) The Duchess of York's <u>ashamed</u> of Richard and says he was a <u>horrible child</u>. She wishes she'd <u>strangled</u> him at birth. That might seem a bit rough coming from your own <u>mother</u>. Richard doesn't care though. He's just <u>sarcastic</u> and <u>rude</u> to her.

2) She's very <u>upset</u> when her <u>sons</u> Clarence and Edward IV <u>die</u>. We can see she loves her <u>grandsons</u> (the young Princes) but they're <u>killed</u> too. No wonder the Duchess <u>curses Richard</u> — just like Lady Anne and Queen Margaret do.

3) By the end of the play the Duchess has <u>had enough</u>. She says she's seen too much trouble and she just wants to <u>die</u>.

<u>Now then, shall I marry the hideous murderer or not..?</u>

If you find yourself shouting "NOOOOO! DON'T MARRY HIM, YOU MUPPET!" at Lady Anne when Richard chats her up, you're not the only one. It's hard to understand why Anne agrees to it.

The Woodvilles and Clarence

The <u>Woodvilles</u> — Rivers, Grey and Dorset — are <u>Queen Elizabeth's relatives</u>.
The Duke of <u>Clarence</u> is <u>Richard's brother</u> (he's older than Richard but younger than Edward IV).

The Woodvilles Have a Hard Time of it

1) Richard <u>doesn't like</u> the Woodvilles. He's annoyed that they've become <u>powerful</u> now that Elizabeth is Queen.

2) Earl <u>Rivers</u> looks after his <u>sister</u>, Queen Elizabeth. He offers her <u>good advice</u>, e.g. it's his idea to get young Prince Edward crowned as soon as possible after King Edward IV's death. Rivers is <u>suspicious of Richard</u> — just like Elizabeth is.

> Let him be crowned. In him your comfort lives.
> Drown desperate sorrow in dead Edward's grave
> And plant your joys in living Edward's throne.
> Act 2, Scene 2, 98-100

3) The Woodvilles know their <u>duty</u>. Edward IV tells them to make up with their enemies, Hastings and Buckingham, so they do. They're <u>loyal</u> to young Prince Edward as well.

4) <u>Rivers</u> and <u>Grey</u> are imprisoned and <u>killed</u> at Pomfret Castle on Richard's orders. Their friend <u>Sir Thomas Vaughan</u> is executed with them. All three appear to Richard and Richmond as <u>ghosts</u> at the end of the play.

5) Queen Elizabeth's <u>other son</u>, the Marquis of <u>Dorset</u>, gets away. Elizabeth tells Dorset to go abroad and join Richmond. It's a good plan — Richmond wins and <u>Dorset survives</u>.

Clarence Feels Guilty About his Past

1) Clarence has got a <u>dodgy past</u> — he plotted against his brother Edward IV during the Wars of the Roses. Later on he changed back to Edward's side. He feels bad about it though. He <u>says sorry</u> for his treason before he dies.

> I'm not a pheasant plucker
> I'm a pheasant plucker's mate
> And I'm only plucking pheasants
> Cos the pheasant plucker's late.

2) Clarence is <u>good with words</u>. He has a horrible <u>nightmare</u> about drowning and he describes it in vivid detail. He talks one of the <u>murderers</u> out of killing him, but then the other one kills him.

3) He's fooled by Richard's <u>fake sympathy</u>. He doesn't find out Richard has tricked him until the very last minute. It's too late by then of course.

4) Clarence cares deeply about his <u>family</u>. He pleads for them not to be <u>punished</u> for his mistakes.

> Yet execute thy wrath in me alone.
> Oh, spare my guiltless wife and my poor children.
> Act 1, Scene 4, 71-72

5) He has a horrible <u>death</u>. He's <u>stabbed</u> then <u>drowned</u> in a barrel of wine.

Grey's a colourful character...

So that's another four victims of Richard then: Rivers, Grey, Vaughan and Clarence. At least Dorset gets away in time. There's a lot to be said for taking good advice when someone offers it.

The Nobles

This lot are a bunch of <u>Lords</u> and <u>Dukes</u> who have to choose whether to be on <u>Richard's side</u> or not. It's pretty <u>dangerous</u> either way.

Buckingham is Richard's Sidekick

1) The Duke of <u>Buckingham</u> does a lot to help Richard become King. Buckingham's cunning and happy to <u>lie</u> and <u>trick people</u>. He pretends he has to <u>persuade</u> Richard to accept the position of King and does a stirring <u>speech</u> about what a brilliant ruler Richard will be.

Honestly, Richard's lovely. You just don't know him like I do.

2) Buckingham is <u>ambitious</u> and he trusts Richard to <u>reward</u> him for his help. Richard <u>flatters him</u> and calls him "my other self". Buckingham gets a little too <u>pleased with himself</u>.

3) Buckingham has his <u>limits</u>. He's not sure about the plan to <u>murder the Princes</u> and so Richard turns against him. Buckingham tries to <u>run away</u> but he ends up being <u>executed</u>. We finally see a decent side to Buckingham when he admits that he <u>deserves to die</u>.

Hastings Underestimates Richard — Big Mistake

1) Lord <u>Hastings</u> doesn't understand how dangerous Richard is. He thinks Richard and Buckingham like him and he says Richard is so <u>honest</u> that you can always tell what he's thinking. The audience knows Hastings is <u>wrong</u>.

2) Hastings is <u>loyal</u> to Edward IV and the young Prince Edward, which is why he <u>won't support</u> Richard to be King. You can <u>admire</u> him for that — but it doesn't do him much good.

3) Hastings is very <u>foolish</u>. He ignores a warning from Stanley that he should get away from Richard, and he's shocked when Richard suddenly orders his <u>execution</u>.

Some Others Help Richard Carry Out his Plans

1) William <u>Catesby</u> does a lot of errands. He's as <u>two-faced</u> as Buckingham and helps to get Richard crowned. Catesby stays <u>loyal to Richard</u> right to the end.

2) Sir Richard <u>Ratcliffe</u> and Lord <u>Lovell</u> do the dirty work. They organise a lot of the <u>executions</u>. Ratcliffe's with Richard at the end and tries to comfort him after his <u>nightmare</u>.

3) Sir Robert <u>Brakenbury</u> is the <u>Lieutenant of the Tower</u>. He has to keep an eye on a lot of Richard's <u>prisoners</u> like Clarence and the young princes.

4) <u>Norfolk</u> and <u>Surrey</u> are on Richard's side but <u>Herbert</u>, <u>Oxford</u> and <u>Blunt</u> fight for Richmond.

"Nobles" in name only then...

There are quite a few of these noblemen, and it's easy to get them mixed up. Buckingham's the most important — if Richard's Mr Burns, then Buckingham's his Smithers. Hastings' plight serves as a warning about how dangerous Richard is — if you don't support him, you'd best be careful.

Richmond and Stanley

These two are the <u>goodies</u> who bring <u>peace</u> to England at the end of the play.
<u>Stanley</u> is <u>Richmond's stepfather</u> — he's married to Richmond's mum.

Richmond *is the* Hero — *he* Kills Richard

1) Henry, Earl of Richmond has a <u>claim to the throne</u> through the <u>Lancastrian</u> side of the Royal Family. He <u>kills Richard III</u> in the Battle of Bosworth at the end of the play and becomes <u>King Henry VII</u>. He puts an end to years of fighting between the Houses of York and Lancaster by bringing the two sides <u>together</u>. He becomes the first <u>Tudor king</u>.

2) Richmond's what a <u>good King</u> should be. He's <u>brave in battle</u> and he gives a good speech to encourage his men. People are <u>loyal</u> to him. The <u>ghosts</u> of Richard's victims all wish him <u>success</u> too.

3) Richmond's quite <u>different</u> from Richard. He's <u>straightforward</u> and he's got a <u>clear conscience</u>. He sleeps well before the battle and is <u>optimistic</u> and <u>confident</u>.

4) People call him "<u>virtuous</u>" and "<u>holy</u>", and he prays to God for success. He wants to win for the sake of <u>peace</u> and justice — <u>not</u> because he's <u>greedy</u> or wants <u>power</u>.

With my winning smile and perfect teeth, I've just got to win. Hurrah!

In God's name, cheerly on, courageous friends,
To reap the harvest of perpetual peace
By this one bloody trial of sharp war.
Act 5, Scene 2, 14-16

Stanley *Secretly* Supports Richmond

1) Lord Stanley is also known as the <u>Earl of Derby</u>. He <u>pretends</u> to be on Richard's side, but <u>secretly</u> sends Richmond <u>messages of support</u>. He gives <u>good advice</u> and encouragement to Richmond.

Ooh, aren't I a tease?

2) Stanley tries to <u>warn Hastings</u> to be careful — but Hastings doesn't listen.

3) Stanley's <u>wise</u> and <u>cautious</u>. Even Richard isn't quite sure <u>whose side</u> he's on. He's one of the few who sees through Richard — but he's <u>clever</u> enough not to speak out against him until the time is right.

4) He wants what's <u>best for the country</u> — not just what's best for himself. He chooses to go and <u>support Richmond</u> even though it means leaving his son George in danger. It's a <u>brave</u> thing to do.

Stanley, don't turn to the dark side...

Richmond turns out to be a very important character, although we don't get to meet him until Act 5. Stanley's an interesting bloke who's lurking around throughout the play, although it's not clear exactly where his loyalties lie until fairly near the end.

The Less Important People

A lot of these people don't say much but play a part in Richard's plans, sometimes without realising.

Some Characters are Involved in Killing People

1) Tyrrel is proud and greedy. He organises the murders of the two young Princes in the Tower of London, but he says afterwards how terrible it was. The two tough guys he got to do it — Dighton and Forrest — actually cried.

Are you sure you're the right Sheriff?

Darn tootin', pardner.

2) There are some officials like the Sheriff. He takes Buckingham to his execution.

3) The Keeper of the Tower has to guard Clarence. He's respectful to him.

4) There are two murderers who come to kill Clarence as well.

Some Characters Talk About What's Happening

1) Three Citizens (ordinary town people) discuss what's going to happen after King Edward IV's death. One of them thinks things will be fine, but another says Prince Edward is too young to rule, and this might cause trouble.

2) The Scrivener has written out the legal charges against Hastings. He tells us that the charges are false, but no one dares say so.

3) The Lord Mayor is fooled by Richard and Buckingham. They tell him that Hastings has been plotting and he believes it. The Mayor also believes it when Richard pretends to be religious as well, and he pleads with Richard to become King.

4) There's a Pursuivant (a royal messenger) who chats to Hastings, and lots of other servants, messengers and pages.

Richard Uses the Church Officials for his Plans

1) The Bishop of Ely goes scurrying off for strawberries when Richard tells him to. Later on he goes over to Richmond's side.

2) The Lord Cardinal (Archbishop of Canterbury) is persuaded by Buckingham to take the young Duke of York away from his mother to join his brother in the Tower.

3) The Archbishop of York is anxious and confused. He helps Queen Elizabeth run off to safety after they hear that her family have been arrested.

4) Sir Christopher Urswick is a priest who takes a letter of support from Stanley to Richmond.

5) There's also a random priest who greets Hastings on his way to the Tower.

Shakespearean pit workers — the miner characters...

Don't worry if you get these characters a bit confused, e.g. if you forget who the strawberry-specialist is. A lot of them, like the murderers, are named after what they do, which helps.

Revision Summary

You need to be confident about who all the characters are and why they're important. There are some pretty complicated relationships in there — once you've sussed out who does what to who, you can get on with writing cracking essays. If you're not clear about this stuff, studying the play will be harder than dragging Dawn French up Mount Snowdon wearing flip-flops. Check you can answer all these questions.

1) How would Shakespeare's audience expect Richard to behave from his appearance?

2) How does Richard act in front of the Mayor?

3) How does Richard let Buckingham down?
   a) He kills Buckingham's brother.
   b) He promises to reward him but doesn't.
   c) He forgets to pick him up from the dentist's.

4) Who's Queen Elizabeth's husband?

5) How does Queen Elizabeth react when Rivers and Grey are arrested?

6) Who's Prince Edward's brother?

7) What happened to Lady Anne's husband?

8) Why does Richard have Lady Anne killed?

9) Why is Queen Margaret so bitter?

10) What does the Duchess of York say Richard was like when he was a child?

11) Who are the Woodvilles?

12) Why does Clarence feel guilty?

13) How does Buckingham help Richard out?
   a) He kills Queen Margaret.
   b) He helps Richard become King.
   c) He gets him tickets for Pop Idol.

14) What happens to Buckingham in the end?

15) What does Hastings reckon Richard and Buckingham think of him?

16) Who's the Lieutenant of the Tower?

17) Who kills Richard at the end?
   a) Richmond
   b) Stanley
   c) Margaret

18) How is Stanley related to Richmond?

19) Who organises the murders of the young Princes?

20) What does the Scrivener think about the charges against Hastings?

21) What part does the Lord Cardinal play in Richard's schemes?

History

Shakespeare wrote Richard III in 1593, when Queen Elizabeth I was on the throne.

The Play is Based on Real History

1) Shakespeare used a lot of characters who really existed. The royal family was real, and so were the Woodvilles, Buckingham, Stanley and Hastings.

2) The play is set in 1485. The Wars of the Roses had been going on for more than 35 years. These were real battles between different branches of the royal family — the House of York and the House of Lancaster. Each House thought they should be ruling the country.

3) Henry VI was a Lancastrian. After his death, Edward IV, who was a Yorkist, became King. After he died, his brother Richard III (also a Yorkist) became King. He was killed at the Battle of Bosworth, and the Earl of Richmond became King Henry VII.

4) Henry VII was a Lancastrian, but he united the two Houses by marrying a Yorkist. He became the first Tudor King, ending the wars.

Shakespeare Changed Some Events

1) Shakespeare made up some things and changed some characters. He wanted to make his play exciting and dramatic.

Maybe I should add some killer robots... No, don't be silly. I've got it — Buckingham leaves to go and live in Perth...

2) For example, the young Princes really did disappear — but there's no proof Richard killed them.

3) The real Queen Margaret had already died by the time the events in the play happened — she didn't really hang on in there cursing people.

Richard III was Probably Not As Bad in Real Life

1) Shakespeare made Richard III come across as pretty evil. People used to believe that if you were bad inside it would show in an ugly appearance. So Shakespeare made him deformed and horrible to look at and gave him a warped personality.

2) Shakespeare also made Richmond a typical good guy. He's the first Tudor King and he only challenges Richard's rule because he wants to rescue England from chaos.

3) Queen Elizabeth I would have been happy with this version, because Richmond was her grandfather. During her reign, it became popular to exaggerate how evil Richard III was.

This is sometimes called the Tudor Myth. It basically means:
Henry VII (Richmond) = good,
Richard III = very, very bad.

One false move and you're history...

Don't worry, you don't need to know all the ins and outs of medieval history. But it's useful to know some background, like the Wars of the Roses, as it helps make sense of what happens in the play.

Fate, Dreams and Omens

Richard III is <u>bound to fail</u> because he becomes King by doing <u>wrong</u>. Shakespeare included lots of omens and prophecies to make it seem even more <u>inevitable</u>.

Richard Thinks he's In Control — but he's Wrong

1) The first prophecy we hear about is one that <u>King Edward IV</u> heard. A wizard told him that someone whose name begins with "<u>G</u>" would <u>murder his heirs</u>. Richard uses this to make Edward suspicious of <u>Clarence</u>, whose first name is <u>George</u>. In fact the "G" stands for <u>Gloucester</u> — Richard is the Duke of Gloucester, and it's <u>Richard</u> who kills them.

2) <u>Henry VI</u> said that <u>Richmond</u> would be king. And an <u>Irish prophet</u> told Richard that he wouldn't live long after he saw Richmond. These prophecies hint that Richard <u>can't win</u> — however confident he seems.

3) The <u>ghosts</u> which appear to Richard and Richmond before the battle confirm this. They tell <u>Richard</u> to <u>despair and die</u> and they tell <u>Richmond</u> to <u>expect victory</u>.

A lot of the Curses we hear Come True

1) <u>Lady Anne curses Richard</u> over the coffin of Henry VI. She also curses his <u>future wife</u> — which turns out to be her. Whoops.

2) <u>Queen Margaret</u> curses the other characters so severely that even <u>Buckingham</u> is frightened.

> My hair doth stand on end to hear her curses.
> Act 1, Scene 3, line 303

MARGARET'S CURSES

- She hopes that Edward IV's son, the young <u>Prince Edward</u>, will <u>die young</u>.
- She wants Queen Elizabeth to see her <u>children die</u>.
- She says that <u>Rivers</u>, <u>Dorset</u> and <u>Hastings</u> will die early.
- She wishes Richard <u>bad dreams</u> and friends who <u>turn against him</u>.

Several Characters have Meaningful Dreams

1) <u>Clarence</u> has a nightmare about Richard <u>pushing him into the sea</u>. Then two murderers — sent by Richard — stab him and <u>drown him</u> in a barrel of wine.

2) <u>Stanley</u> has a dream about how <u>dangerous</u> Richard is. He sends a messenger to <u>warn Hastings</u>, but Hastings laughs at it.

I predict you will pass your exams, oh yes...

Studying the play today, it's tempting to see Margaret's curses as just the rabid ramblings of a mad, bitter old hag. But in Shakespeare's times, they would have been seen as a grim warning.

Crimes, Guilt and Remorse

There's an awful lot of <u>nastiness</u> in this play. Some of the characters come to realise that <u>murdering people</u> just isn't cricket. Richard just <u>ploughs on</u> regardless though.

Bad Deeds <u>Have</u> Bad Consequences

In Shakespeare's time, people had strong ideas about <u>good</u> and <u>evil</u>. Most people in England were <u>Christian</u> and believed that, if you did bad things in this life, your <u>soul would be punished</u> when you died.

Don't say I didn't warn you, sunshine.

The play is full of characters who <u>lie</u>, <u>trick each other</u> and even <u>kill</u>. Shakespeare wanted us to see that they wouldn't be rewarded for it.

Some Characters Feel <u>Guilty</u>

Several characters want to <u>clear their consciences</u> before they die. They hope that if they <u>repent</u> their crimes they will <u>save their souls</u> from being <u>damned forever</u>.

1) Clarence has a horrible <u>dream</u> about drowning. He feels <u>guilty</u> because in the past he <u>fought against his brother</u>, Edward IV. He accepts that <u>God</u> may punish him for that. He prays that his <u>family doesn't suffer</u> for his crime though.

2) The <u>murderers</u> who come to kill Clarence don't find it easy. Clarence warns them that if they kill him they're <u>breaking God's laws</u>. The second murderer talks about his own <u>conscience</u>. He <u>repents</u> almost immediately.

3) <u>Edward IV</u> knows he's <u>going to die</u>. He's keen to <u>do good</u> before he dies so his soul will go to Heaven. He's full of <u>remorse</u> when he hears that Clarence has been killed. He's afraid <u>God</u> will <u>judge</u> them all for it.

4) <u>Dighton</u> and <u>Forrest</u>, who Tyrell gets to kill the Princes, end up <u>weeping with guilt</u>.

5) <u>Buckingham</u> has an attack of conscience too. Just before he's <u>executed</u>, he admits that he has <u>done wrong</u>. He says he deserves to die.

Richard III Isn't Sorry <u>for What He's Done</u>

In for a penny...

1) At the start of the play, Richard <u>boasts</u> about the trouble he's going to cause — and he does it. He <u>chooses</u> to be a <u>villain</u> right to the end.

2) Richard has <u>more</u> to <u>feel guilty</u> about than anyone. He's haunted by the <u>ghosts of his victims</u> just before the battle. He has to <u>face up</u> to what he's done.

3) It's a clear chance to repent. But he <u>rejects his conscience</u> and sticks with his plans.

Sorry is all that you can't say...

You might think that saying sorry just isn't good enough when you've done the things these people have done. But in Richard III, realising you've done wrong is a big thing. The fact that Richard never repents makes him come across as much, much worse than Buckingham or anyone else.

ACT 1 SCENES 1 & 2	# What Happens in Act One

Right then. This is a long old play, so best get down to it and find out what happens.

Scene 1 — Richard Cons Clarence

Before the play starts, the royal houses of <u>York</u> and <u>Lancaster</u> have been at war. The Lancastrian King Henry VI and his son Prince Edward have been <u>killed</u> by Richard, a <u>Yorkist</u>. Now Richard's brother, Edward IV, is King, and the Yorkists are back in <u>power</u>. But the troubles are far from over...

1 The wars are over, but Richard's not happy
England is at peace, and now Edward IV, Richard's older brother, is King. But peace and happiness don't suit Richard — he says he's ugly and deformed, and determined to cause trouble. He tells us that he's turned King Edward and his other brother, the Duke of Clarence, against each other. Lines 1-41

2 Richard tells Clarence he'll stick up for him
Clarence enters on his way to being imprisoned in the Tower of London. Richard pretends to be surprised and asks why Clarence is being imprisoned, and Clarence says he doesn't know. Richard then tells Clarence that it's not the King who's behind it, but his wife, Queen Elizabeth. Richard then tells Clarence that he'll stick up for him and get him freed (he's lying). The guard leads Clarence away, then Richard reveals he's actually going to have Clarence killed. Lines 42-120

He ain't heavy... he's my brother.

3 Hastings tells Richard the King is ill
Hastings arrives and tells Richard that King Edward is sick and the doctors are very worried. Hastings leaves. Richard talks about his plan to get Clarence killed, and then marry Lady Anne. When King Edward IV dies, Richard wants to take his place. Lines 121-162

No one else hears Richard say this — it's his and our secret.

Scene 2 — Richard Chats Anne Up

1 Anne mourns for her husband and father-in-law
Anne follows the body of the former King, Henry VI, which is on its way to being buried. She mourns for him and for her husband, his son Prince Edward. Lines 1-32

2 Richard tries to woo Anne, but she resists
Richard enters and orders the procession to stop. Anne curses him, saying he killed Henry VI and Prince Edward. At first Richard denies it, then admits it. He cleverly tries to talk his way into Anne's affections, by saying that he killed them because Anne was so beautiful and he was in love with her. She spits at him and continues to curse him. Lines 33-150

3 Richard wins her over
Richard makes a speech about how he never cries, but he cries when he looks at Anne. He hands her his sword and tells her to kill him if she doesn't want him, but she won't kill him. He gives her a ring, and eventually manages to convince Anne to leave the procession and meet up with him later on. Lines 151-226

4 Richard congratulates himself
Richard reflects on what he has achieved, winning over Anne despite being ugly and having killed her husband and father-in-law. Lines 227-263

What do you get if you cross a leopard with Richard III?

Spotted Dick. Anyway, there you have it — all the fun of the first two scenes. Use these pages to <u>get to know the story</u> and your key scenes should start to make a whole lot more sense.

What Happens in Act One

Here's the rest of Act 1. I hope you haven't become too fond of Clarence...

Scene 3 — *Margaret Curses Everyone*

In this scene, the <u>bitter</u> old Queen Margaret (Henry VI's widow) enters the fray.
She causes a lot of trouble, but that sly old dog Richard uses this to his <u>advantage</u>.

1 Queen Elizabeth's relatives comfort her
Rivers and Grey try to cheer Queen Elizabeth up by telling her the King will be better soon. She's worried about the prospect of Richard becoming her son's Protector when the King dies. Stanley (Earl of Derby) and Buckingham arrive and report that the King is on the mend and is keen to sort out the quarrels between Richard and the Queen's family. Lines 1-41

2 Richard starts an argument
Richard enters and claims that people have been spreading lies about him, Clarence and Hastings. Elizabeth says he's just jealous because her family has come into power. Lines 42-109

3 Queen Margaret has a go at everyone
Margaret sneaks in and hides unseen from the other characters. She says to herself that Elizabeth has taken her rightful position of Queen, and says Richard is a murderer. Lines 110-156

Richard's only pretending to be sympathetic with Margaret. It adds to his image of being a simple, straight-up bloke. He's secretly quite happy about the upset Margaret's caused.

4 Margaret causes a stir
Margaret comes forward and says the others are all fighting over what is hers. She warns them about Richard, but Elizabeth won't listen. Margaret predicts that Elizabeth will wish she had listened to her. She tries to be friendly to Buckingham, but he sides with Richard. Margaret curses them all and leaves. Richard defends Margaret, then Catesby comes to call them all over to see the King. Lines 157-322

5 Richard plans more trouble
Richard reflects on his plan to blame Clarence's imprisonment on Queen Elizabeth's relatives (Rivers, Grey and Dorset), and to set Stanley, Hastings and Buckingham against them for it. Two murderers enter and Richard gives them instructions to kill Clarence. Lines 323-354

Scene 4 — *Clarence is Murdered*

Poor old Clarence almost talks his way out of it — but there's <u>no stopping</u> Richard's schemes.

1 Clarence describes a bad dream
In the Tower, Clarence tells his keeper that he's had a horrible dream. He dreamt that he and Richard were on a ship, Richard slipped and pushed him overboard, and that he drowned, and went to hell. The keeper stays with Clarence while he sleeps. Lines 1-75

2 The murderers come to Clarence
Brakenbury enters. The murderers enter and give Brakenbury a warrant instructing him to leave Clarence in their charge. Brakenbury and the keeper leave. One of the murderers has doubts about killing Clarence, but the other murderer reminds him of the money and he agrees to go through with it. Lines 76-152

3 Clarence tries to talk them out of it, but is killed
Clarence wakes up and sees the murderers. He thinks that Edward has sent them. He manages to talk one of them out of killing him, but the other stabs him from behind, then drowns him in a wine barrel. Lines 153-278

ACT 2 SCENES 1-4

What Happens in Act Two

Here's the whole of Act 2. By this point, Richard's really starting to take control. Boo, hiss.

Scene 1 — All's Going Well... then Richard Turns Up

Richard wants <u>conflict</u>, so he sabotages the King's efforts to make peace.

1 King Edward gets everyone to make friends
Queen Elizabeth and her relatives make their peace with Buckingham and Hastings. The King, who is ill, is happy about this. Lines 1-44

2 Richard tells them Clarence is dead
Richard arrives and pretends to make friends with everyone too. Then he tells them that Clarence is dead, and everyone is astonished. Richard says that the King's reversal of the death sentence came too late. Lines 45-95

3 The King is distraught
The King is very upset at the death of Clarence, and asks why no one tried to talk him out of ordering Clarence's death. Richard tells Buckingham that Clarence's death was the fault of Queen Elizabeth's relatives. Lines 96-141

Come on guys, where's the love?

Scene 2 — The King is Dead

Prince Edward is only a child. If he becomes King, Richard will be his <u>Lord Protector</u> — which means he's in charge.

1 Clarence's kids ask some awkward questions
Clarence's two children ask the Duchess of York, their grandmother, about their father's death. Clarence's son says that Richard told him it was Elizabeth's fault, but the Duchess says Richard is a liar. Lines 1-33

2 Elizabeth announces that the King is dead
Queen Elizabeth arrives with her relatives, Rivers and Dorset, and tells them that King Edward IV is dead. They reflect on the deaths of Clarence and the King. Rivers reminds Elizabeth that her young son, Prince Edward, will now be King. Lines 34-95

3 Buckingham sends for Prince Edward
Richard and Buckingham arrive, and Buckingham orders for a small group of people to be sent to fetch the young Prince Edward to be crowned as King. Then Buckingham tells Richard that he'll arrange for the Prince to be separated from Elizabeth's relatives. Lines 96-154

Scene 3 — Some Citizens Chat About England's Future

Three citizens (ordinary people) discuss the recent news
One citizen says things will be fine under the new King. Another citizen says that Richard is dangerous, and likely to quarrel with Elizabeth's family. He says that having a child as King will cause trouble.

The Woodvilles are Queen Elizabeth's family.

Scene 4 — The Woodvilles are Arrested

1 The young Duke of York talks about Prince Edward
The Archbishop of York, the old Duchess of York, Elizabeth and the young Duke of York chat about the arrival of young Prince Edward. Lines 1-37

2 A messenger brings bad news
Rivers, Grey and Vaughan have been arrested by Richard and Buckingham. Elizabeth realises her family is in danger and she and the young Duke go to sanctuary, where they are safer. Lines 38-73

Section 4 — Understanding The Story

What Happens in Act Three

Richard really starts to get a taste for murder in this act. If only Taggart was around.

Scene 1 — The Young Princes Arrive

1 Prince Edward isn't happy
The young Prince Edward is unhappy that his relatives are not with him. Richard tells him they are evil people, but the Prince isn't convinced. Hastings reports that Elizabeth is holding the Prince's brother, the young Duke of York, in sanctuary. Buckingham orders Cardinal Bourchier to fetch them by force. Lines 1-60

2 Richard, Prince Edward and the Duke of York have a chat
Richard suggests that Prince Edward should stay in the Tower for a few days. The two of them talk for a while, and Richard comments to himself on the Prince's cleverness. Then the young Duke of York arrives, and he too demonstrates his wit. Then the two Princes reluctantly go off to the Tower. Lines 61-150

3 Buckingham and Richard do more plotting
Buckingham sends Catesby to find out whether Hastings will support Richard's bid to be King. Richard tells Buckingham that if Hastings won't support him, he'll have him killed. Then Richard promises Buckingham he'll be made Earl of Hereford when Richard becomes King. Lines 151-200

Scene 2 — Hastings Ignores Stanley's Warning

Hastings <u>won't listen</u> to Stanley's friendly word of advice. Uh-oh.

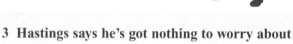

I've never felt less likely to be executed in all my life...

1 A messenger arrives
Hastings is woken by a messenger from Stanley. He warns Hastings of the danger from Richard and suggests they go north together. Hastings says there's nothing to worry about and sends the messenger away. Lines 1-34

2 Hastings tells Catesby he won't support Richard
Catesby arrives and tells Hastings that Elizabeth's relatives are to be killed. Catesby asks Hastings if he'll support Richard's claim to be King — Hastings says he won't. Lines 35-56

3 Hastings says he's got nothing to worry about
Hastings tells Catesby that he's mates with Richard and Buckingham. Stanley enters and points out to Hastings that the same thing could happen to them as to Elizabeth's family. But Hastings says that they're perfectly safe because Richard likes them. Hastings then speaks to some other people, including Buckingham, who knows that Hastings will be killed. Lines 57-123

This is dramatic irony (see p.42). The audience knows that Richard's perfectly prepared to have Hastings killed. He should've listened to Stanley...

Scene 3 — The Woodvilles are Taken to be Killed

The doomed prisoners remember Margaret's curse
Ratcliffe leads Rivers, Grey and Vaughan to their execution. Grey says that Margaret's curse on them is coming true. Rivers hopes it comes true for Richard, Buckingham and Hastings too.

Richard's ma-king me a bit nervous...

I'm beginning to see a pattern here. Clarence was in Richard's way. He got killed. The Woodvilles were awkward. They got killed... Ah well, I'm sure he knows what he's doing.

**ACT 3
SCENES 4-7**

What Happens in Act Three

Scene 4 — It All Goes Wrong for Hastings

1 Prince Edward's coronation is discussed

Hastings, Buckingham, Stanley and the Bishop of Ely meet to discuss the date of the coronation. The Bishop asks Buckingham's opinion, but Buckingham says that Hastings is closer to Richard than him. Richard enters and privately tells Buckingham that he's going to have Hastings killed. Hastings fails to see what's going on and says that Richard seems to be happy. Lines 1-57

> Oops.

2 Richard tricks Hastings

Richard says there's been a plot against him, and Hastings says whoever's behind it deserves to be killed. Richard says it's Elizabeth and Mistress Shore (Hastings' mistress) and orders the execution of Hastings. Hastings wishes he'd listened to Stanley's warnings. He realises Margaret's curse against him has come true. Ratcliffe and Lovell lead him away. Lines 58-107

> Richard can't just kill Hastings for no clear reason, so he makes it look like he's a traitor.

Scene 5 — Richard Prepares to Become King

> Help! We're under attack!

> Well I'm convinced. There's no way this is a trick, none at all.

1 Richard and Buckingham pretend to be under attack

Dressed up in armour, Richard and Buckingham make out to the Mayor that there's been a plot against them and that they're in danger of their lives. Lovell and Ratcliffe come in with Hastings' head. Richard pretends to be sad that Hastings is dead, but says he had no choice but to have him killed. The Mayor is fooled and goes to explain the situation to the citizens. Lines 1-71

2 Richard puts the final touches to his plan to be King

Richard tells Buckingham to tell the citizens that Edward's children, the young Princes, are illegitimate, meaning Richard should be King. Lines 72-109

Scene 6 — A Scrivener Speaks

A scrivener realises what's going on

A scrivener (legal writer) looks over a document accusing Hastings of being a traitor. He realises that the accusation is false, as he was given it the previous night, before Hastings was accused.

Scene 7 — Richard Becomes King

1 The citizens aren't keen

Buckingham tells Richard that he's tried to persuade the citizens of Richard's right to be King, but they weren't very enthusiastic about it. Buckingham tells Richard to pretend to be praying for when the Mayor arrives. Lines 1-55

2 Richard pretends to be reluctant

The Mayor and Catesby arrive. Catesby is sent to ask Richard to be King. Richard pretends to be busy praying and says he doesn't want to be King. Buckingham (who's in on the trick) and the Mayor (who isn't) eventually persuade Richard that he must become King. Lines 56-247

What Happens in Act Four

OK, so Richard's an evil murderer hell-bent on power. But surely he's good with children?

Scene 1 — The Visitors are Denied Access to the Princes

1 Brakenbury says Elizabeth, Anne and the Duchess can't see the young Princes

Queen Elizabeth, the Duchess of York, Dorset and Lady Anne meet on their way to visit Prince Edward and the young Duke of York in the Tower. Then Brakenbury appears and tells them Richard won't allow it. The women protest but Brakenbury isn't having any of it. Stanley arrives to summon Anne to be crowned as Richard's Queen. Lines 1-27

2 Elizabeth, Anne and the Duchess are worried

The women realise that Richard is up to no good. Anne wishes she'd never agreed to marry Richard and says he will have her killed. The Duchess tells Dorset to leave and join Richmond, who is forming an army to fight Richard. The Duchess also tells Anne to go to Richard and Elizabeth to go to sanctuary. Lines 28-103

Scene 2 — King Richard Plans More Murders

1 The new King plots to kill the two young Princes

The newly crowned King Richard III takes the throne. He wants Prince Edward and the young Duke of York dead, and asks for Buckingham's help. Buckingham isn't sure and goes away to think about it. Lines 1-31

2 Richard hires Tyrrel to kill the Princes and plans Anne's death too

Richard sends a page to fetch a man called Tyrrel to kill the Princes. Stanley tells Richard that Dorset has gone to join forces with Richmond. Richard tells Catesby to tell people that his wife Anne is sick and about to die. Tyrrel arrives and Richard gives him instructions to kill the Princes. Lines 32-81

He wants Anne dead so he can marry his niece (Queen Elizabeth's daughter, Elizabeth) to strengthen his position as King.

3 Buckingham's out of favour

Buckingham returns and asks for the reward Richard promised him, but Richard keeps ignoring him. Buckingham remembers that Richard had Hastings killed when he fell out with him, and realises he has to get away from Richard before the same thing happens to him. Lines 82-121

Scene 3 — The Young Princes are Dead

1 The Princes are dead

Tyrrel says the people he hired to kill the Princes almost changed their minds before going through with the murders. Then he tells Richard the Princes are dead. Richard says that Anne too is now dead, so he can go after his niece Elizabeth, but he is worried that Richmond also wants to marry her. Lines 1-43

2 Richard prepares for battle

Ratcliffe brings news of how Richmond and Buckingham are raising armies in Brittany in France against Richard. Richard tells Ratcliffe to gather soldiers for his army. Lines 44-57

Stop it, you're killing me...

At least now Dickie's started killing a few people, it's easier to remember who everyone is. You can't help feeling sorry for the kids, but Hastings — he's just stupid and deserves it if you ask me.

ACT 4 SCENES 4 & 5	# What Happens in Act Four

He may be King now, but things start getting a bit sticky for Dickie from now on.

Scene 4 — Richard Prepares for Battle

1 Margaret says "I told you so"
Margaret listens in on Elizabeth and the Duchess of York discussing how miserable they are about what's happened to their families. Then Margaret comes forward and takes satisfaction in having been right about their downfalls. Lines 1-125

2 Elizabeth and the Duchess have a go at Richard
Richard enters and Queen Elizabeth and the Duchess remind him of the murders he has committed. The Duchess says he will have a violent death. Lines 126-196

3 Richard asks Elizabeth to help him marry her daughter
Richard wants to marry Queen Elizabeth's daughter, also called Elizabeth, and asks her to help him. At first Elizabeth refuses, saying her daughter would never marry Richard because he has killed so many members of her family. Lines 197-290

Now who's mad?

4 Richard seems to convince Elizabeth
Richard says he can't change what he's done in the past, but says he can make up for Queen Elizabeth's sorrow at not having a son as King by making her daughter his Queen. They have a long argument, and Elizabeth mockingly reminds Richard of how untrustworthy he is. Eventually, though, he seems to convince her, and she leaves. Lines 291-430

5 Richard distrusts Stanley
Ratcliffe reports that Richmond's army is sailing from France and will be joined by Buckingham's army. Richard sends Catesby to the Duke of Norfolk to tell him to raise an army. Stanley arrives and tells Richard that Richmond is sailing to England to try and become King. Richard tells Stanley to summon his friends to Richard's side. Richard thinks Stanley might betray him and help Richmond instead, so he holds Stanley's son, George, as a hostage, to ensure Stanley's loyalty. Lines 431-497

6 Some messengers bring bad news
Three messengers announce there are armies ready to fight Richard in various parts of England, but another says that Buckingham's army has split up and Buckingham has disappeared. Catesby says that Buckingham has been captured, but Richmond has landed with a strong army. Richard says they have to stop talking and prepare for battle. Lines 498-538

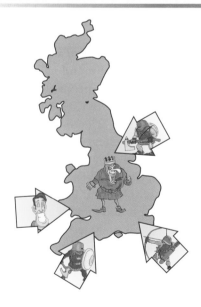

Scene 5 — Stanley Secretly Sends Richmond his Support

Stanley double-crosses Richard — he'll have to be careful.

Stanley sends Richmond a message
Stanley tells Sir Christopher Urswick to tell Richmond that he can't openly support him because Richard is holding his son hostage. But he says to tell him that Queen Elizabeth wants her daughter to marry Richmond. Stanley gives Sir Christopher a letter assuring Richmond that he is on his side.

What Happens in Act Five

Ooh it's the last act, I'm all excited. But look out, there's ghosts in this bit...

Scene 1 — Buckingham's for the Chop

Buckingham is led to his execution
The sheriff takes Buckingham to be killed, telling him Richard won't speak with him. Buckingham realises he's getting what he deserves, and remembers Margaret's prophecy.

So Margaret was right about me too. Pants.

Scene 2 — Richmond's Feeling Confident

We've heard all about him — now Richmond finally makes an appearance.

Right, chaps, let's kick some hunchback bottom.

Richmond marches to battle
Richmond and his supporters are marching towards battle, and are only one day's march away from Richard. Richmond has received Stanley's letter of support, and he's feeling good.

Scene 3 — The Night Before Battle

1 Richard and Richmond set up camp
Richard's side pitch their tent in Bosworth field, ready for the battle the next morning. Richard says their army is three times as big as Richmond's. Nearby, Richmond arrives with his followers. He sends Blunt to find Stanley and give him a note. Lines 1-45

2 Richard sends for Stanley
It is the evening before the battle and Richard is feeling tense. He tells Catesby to send for Stanley's regiment, then talks with Ratcliffe about preparations for the battle. Lines 46-79

3 Stanley talks secretly with Richmond
Stanley wishes Richmond good luck, but explains that he cannot be seen supporting him because of Stanley's son being held hostage. Richmond prays then sleeps. Lines 80-118

4 The Ghosts of Richard's victims visit Richard and Richmond
The ghosts of the people Richard has murdered come to Richard and Richmond in their dreams — first the older Prince Edward, then Henry VI, Clarence, Rivers, Grey and Vaughan, Hastings, the two young Princes, Anne and finally Buckingham. The ghosts wish despair and death on Richard, and success and victory on Richmond. Richard wakes up terrified and feels haunted by his conscience. Ratcliffe comes to tell Richard the battle is about to begin. Lines 119-223

5 Richmond and Richard rouse their troops
Richmond wakes after having pleasant dreams. He gives an oration (speech) to his soldiers. Then Richard gives his oration to his troops. A messenger tells Richard that Stanley won't support him. Richard orders the death of Stanley's son, but there isn't time before the battle. Lines 224-352

Richard and Richmond use these speeches to motivate their troops before the big battle — doubtless accompanied by lots of "hurrahs" and "huzzahs".

ACT 5 SCENES 4 & 5 — *What Happens in Act Five*

Nearly finished. I wonder how it'll end — maybe there'll be a really surprising twist...
Nope, the good guy wins. Never saw that coming.

Scene 4 — *The Battle*

He may be a scheming, dishonest murderer, but Richard's a <u>brave fighter</u>.

Richard looks for Richmond

In the midst of battle, Catesby and Norfolk come across Richard. His horse has been killed, but he's desperate for another one so he can go and fight Richmond, after having already killed five other men dressed like him. Catesby advises him to flee, but Richard is determined to fight Richmond.

COME ON THEN!

This is where Richard says the famous line "A horse, a horse, my kingdom for a horse!" In fact, he says it twice — it's that good.

Scene 5 — *Richmond Defeats Richard*

Richard finally meets his <u>end</u> — and not a second too soon.

1 Richmond kills Richard

Richard and Richmond fight, and Richmond kills Richard. Stanley congratulates him and presents him with the crown, taken from Richard's head. Stanley tells us that his son is safe and well. Lines 1-14

2 Richmond looks forward to peace

In the closing speech, Richmond says he will bring together the warring sides of the royal family. He says he'll unite the houses of York and Lancaster by marrying the Yorkist Princess Elizabeth (Richmond is a Lancastrian), so that England can be peaceful again. Lines 15-41

Now let's jolly well live in peace together, what?

That's all folks...

Come on, admit it, it's not that boring. There's loads of action, and all that double-dealing certainly keeps it interesting. If you ever get in a muddle while you're reading the play, you can always have a look back at this section to work out what's happening. Now, unto the exam, and victory! Ahem.

Revision Summary

I told you it was a long play. It's complicated too, and right now you're probably feeling exhausted just from trying to follow it. But it'll all click into place in time. And luckily for you, I've written loads of questions about what happens, so you can see what you know and what you don't. Take a deep breath and dive in.

1) Who were the two sides in the Wars of the Roses?
   a) The Houses of York and Lancaster.
   b) Britain and France.
   c) Chelsea and Arsenal.

2) What's the "Tudor Myth"?

3) What's the first prophecy mentioned in the play?

4) What does Queen Margaret say about the young Prince Edward?

5) When does Buckingham realise he's done wrong?

6) How does Richard react to his chance to repent?

7) Who's the King at the start of the play?

8) Who's being led to the Tower in Act 1, Scene 1?

9) Who does Richard blame Clarence's imprisonment on?

10) Who is Anne mourning for when Richard interrupts her?

11) What does Clarence dream about before he's murdered?
    a) The deaths of the young Princes.
    b) Drowning and going to hell.
    c) A tractor made of spaghetti.

12) How does Richard ruin King Edward IV's attempts to create peace?

13) Why would Richard gain more power if Prince Edward became King?

14) Which characters are arrested in Act 2, Scene 4?

15) What does Richard promise Buckingham as a reward for his support?

16) What's Hastings' reaction to Stanley's warning?

17) How does Richard trick Hastings in Act 3, Scene 4?

18) Who does Richard get to tell the people that the young Princes are illegitimate?

19) Why does the Scrivener reckon the accusation against Hastings is dodgy?

20) What's Richard doing when the Mayor comes to ask him to be King?

21) Who prevents the women from visiting the young Princes in the Tower?

22) What's Buckingham's response when Richard asks for his support in killing the young Princes?

23) What does Richard ask of Queen Elizabeth in Act 4, Scene 4?

24) How does Richard try to make sure Stanley's loyal to him?

25) What does Stanley tell Richmond in his message in Act 4, Scene 5?

26) What effect do the ghosts have on Richard and Richmond?

27) Why does Richard want a horse in Act 5, Scene 4?

28) What does Richmond say he's going to do after becoming King?

Planning and Structure

If you <u>plan</u> your essay first, you'll have <u>more</u> chance of getting <u>loads</u> of <u>marks</u>.

Before you Write, *Make a Plan*

I wish I was organised...

Planning means <u>organising</u> your material to help you write a clear answer that makes sense. A good plan turns that <u>heap of ideas</u> in your head into an <u>argument</u> supported by <u>points</u>.

> Planning might seem a <u>pain</u> to do, but if you do it, you'll be <u>less</u> likely to get <u>lost</u> halfway through the essay.

You Need a *Beginning*, a *Middle* and an *End*

> A good essay has a <u>beginning</u>, a <u>middle</u> and an <u>end</u>. Just like a good story.

Middle

End   Beginning

Just like me then.

1) The <u>hardest</u> part is <u>beginning</u> your essay. The <u>first sentence</u> has to start <u>answering</u> the question, and tell the examiner that your essay is going to be good. All that from <u>one</u> sentence — so you'd better start <u>practising</u>.

2) The middle part of your essay <u>develops</u> your <u>argument</u> — this is where you make all your points. Follow your plan.

3) The end <u>sums up</u> the points you've made and <u>rounds</u> the essay <u>off</u> nicely.

Five Steps *to Planning a Good Essay*

1) Work out <u>exactly</u> what the question is asking you to do. Find the <u>key words</u> and circle them.

2) Read the <u>set scenes</u> — highlight <u>quotations</u> you could use.

3) Jot down your <u>ideas</u> — from the set scenes they <u>give</u> you, and from your <u>knowledge</u> of the <u>rest</u> of the play — and then put them into an <u>order</u>.

4) Decide what your <u>opinion</u> is, and how you can <u>use</u> your points to <u>support</u> it — to form an <u>argument</u>. Put your <u>best</u> point <u>first</u>.

5) Don't stick to your plan <u>rigidly</u>. If you think of any more <u>good ideas</u> once you've started writing, then try to fit them in.

It's the beginning of the end...

If you're not sure what your <u>opinion</u> is, state the arguments <u>for and against</u>, and give evidence to support each viewpoint. Answer the question by <u>comparing</u> the views on <u>each side</u>.

Planning and Structure

Here are a few more handy tips which will help you in the exam...

Making Your Plan

The example in the box shows the kind of thing you could write for a plan. Don't bother writing in proper English — just get your ideas down.

This essay's all about Richard. Make notes on everything you think is relevant from the scene — concentrate on the bits where Richard is speaking.

Decide on the best order to write about your points in.

Write down any comments you've got on what happens.

Scribble down good quotes to back it all up.

> What do we learn about the character of Richard in Act 1 Scene 2?
>
> 1. He's very persuasive He persuades Anne to marry him, despite being "misshapen" and having killed her husband and father-in-law.
>
> 3. 2. He's proud of his skills At the end of the scene, he is very pleased with himself for winning Anne against all the odds — "was ever woman in this humour won?"
>
> 2. 3. He is very determined Anne isn't easily won over — she seems disgusted with him, saying he's "unfit for any place but hell". But Richard isn't put off and keeps talking until he convinces her.

Think About Style and Vocabulary

1) Use interesting words — the examiner will get bored if you overuse dull words and phrases like "nice" and "I think". Try using words like "fascinating" and phrases like "in my opinion".

2) Keep your style formal — this makes your argument more convincing and gets you even more marks.

3) If you think a passage is "poetic", "realistic" etc., remember to explain exactly why — with examples. Don't assume it's obvious to the examiner.

Keep bearing in mind the words used in the question. Using them in your essay will show you're keeping to the task and not getting lost.

My essay blossomed — I plant it well...

Don't just launch straight in — take the time to plan. Once you've jotted some ideas down, you'll realise you have more to say than you thought — so there's less reason to panic. And let's face it, a structured essay will get more marks than one that goes all over the place...

Writing Your Answer

Once you've got a plan, you're <u>ready</u> to start writing.
Make your points as <u>clearly</u> as you can so the examiner knows what you're on about.

Write a Simple Opening Paragraph

Start by using the exact <u>words of the task</u> in your introduction.

Your introduction <u>doesn't</u> have to be <u>long</u> at all. It's just there to show what your <u>basic</u> <u>answer</u> to the task is. In the rest of the paragraphs you'll need to go into <u>detail</u>.

 e.g. *What do we learn about the character of Richard in Act 1, Scene 2?*

In this scene, we <u>learn</u> several things about <u>Richard</u>. In successfully wooing Anne, Richard shows that he is a clever, determined <u>character</u> who is proud of his skills.

The first thing we notice here is how persuasive he is...

The opening sentences use words from the <u>question</u>.

Once you've written your opening paragraph, just follow the order of the <u>plan</u> to write the rest of your essay.

Use Lots of Tasty Quotations

<u>Quotes</u> show where your answer comes from. You're <u>guaranteed</u> to get better marks if your answer's got some good quotes. Here's how to <u>quote properly</u>.

Start a new <u>paragraph</u>.

e.g. *Richard admits that he killed Henry VI and his son Edward, but convinces Anne that he did it because of her beauty:*
"'twas I that stabbed young Edward —
But 'twas thy heavenly face that set me on."
Act 1, Scene 2, 181-182

Copy down the <u>exact</u> words.

Say <u>where</u> the quote comes from. Give the <u>act</u>, <u>scene</u>, and <u>line numbers</u>.

Don't quote <u>more</u> than <u>two or three</u> lines at a time.

If the quote's less than a line you <u>won't</u> need to put it in a separate paragraph or say where the quote's from, but you <u>will</u> need to put it in quotation marks.

Richard congratulates himself on the fact that Anne now sees him as "a marvellous proper man".

"Salt and Vinegar" — there's a tasty quote...

The examiners really are <u>dead keen</u> on quoting. If you don't quote at all, you'll get a <u>low mark</u>, no matter <u>how good</u> the <u>rest</u> of your answer is. Don't quote <u>huge chunks</u>, though — you only need a <u>couple of lines</u> to show where your answer comes from. It's all about striking a balance.

<u>Concluding and Checking for Errors</u>

Once you've made <u>all</u> your points, you need to <u>sum up</u> your answer and <u>check</u> it through.

<u>Summing Up — Bringing Together the Key Points</u>

The conclusion to my speech will be very concise — barely half an hour...

1) Start a new <u>paragraph</u> by going back to the <u>original question</u>.

2) Restate the <u>main points</u> of your essay <u>briefly</u>. This makes it clear how you've <u>answered</u> the question.

3) Don't go on and on, though. You must be <u>focused</u>. Once you've <u>summed up</u>, write a final <u>sentence</u> to <u>conclude</u>.

<u>Go Over Your Essay When You've Finished</u>

1) Try to <u>leave time</u> at the end to <u>read through</u> your essay quickly. Check that it <u>makes sense</u>, that you haven't got any facts wrong, and that it says what you <u>want</u> it to say.

2) Check the <u>grammar</u>, <u>spelling</u> and <u>punctuation</u>. If you find a <u>mistake</u>, put <u>brackets</u> round it, cross it out <u>neatly</u> with two lines through it and write the <u>correction</u> above.

How many more times do I have to go over it?

> determined
> Richard is (~~diturmined~~) to be King

Don't <u>scribble</u> or put <u>whitener</u> on mistakes — it looks <u>messy</u> and you'll <u>lose marks</u>.

3) If you've written something which isn't <u>clear</u>, put an <u>asterisk</u> * at the end of the sentence. Put another asterisk in the <u>margin</u> beside the sentence, and write what you <u>mean</u> in the margin.

> *He holds his son hostage. | Richard does not trust Stanley*.

<u>Don't Panic if You Realise You've Gone Wrong</u>

If you realise you've <u>forgotten</u> something really <u>obvious</u> and <u>easy</u>, then write a <u>note</u> about it at the bottom of the <u>final</u> page, to tell the Examiner. If there's time, write an extra <u>paragraph</u>. You'll pick up marks for <u>noticing</u> your mistake.

> <u>Don't give up</u> if you're running out of <u>time</u> — even if you only have <u>five minutes</u> left, that's still time to pick up <u>extra marks</u>.

<u>Check, check, check — I must be rich...</u>

You've almost <u>finished</u>. Keep your conclusions <u>to the point</u>, and <u>check</u> your essay so you don't <u>throw away</u> marks on <u>silly mistakes</u>. Keep a <u>clear head</u> right up to the end — then it's <u>teatime</u>.

Revision Summary

I like to think of it as the 5 Ps — Planning Prevents Pitifully Poor Performance. Actually, I think it's a bit more positive than that — Planning Provides Practically Perfect Performance. The main point is Planning Planning Planning Planning Planning. Anyway, that's enough Ps for now. On with the revision summary — you only know the answers when you don't have to flick back.

1) What's the big advantage of making a plan for an essay question?

2) What are the three vital ingredients of a good plan?
   a) Spelling, handwriting and punctuation.
   b) Great ideas, brilliant ideas and fantastic ideas.
   c) A beginning, a middle and an end.

3) If you have a great idea when you're writing your essay which wasn't on your original plan, is it OK to fit it into your essay anyway?

4) Put these steps in order:
   • write down good quotes
   • read the scene (or scenes)
   • make a plan

How do you spell "clueless"?

5) What do you use quotes for when you're writing an essay?

6) Is it OK to use lots of slang in the exam?

7) What do you have to do with the first sentence of the answer?
   a) Give a general answer to the question.
   b) Make your best point straightaway.
   c) Put in a really interesting quote.

8) What three bits of information do you have to give after any quote that's more than a line long?

9) What punctuation marks do you use on quotes that are shorter than one line?

10) How long should your closing paragraph be?
    a) About half a page.
    b) As long as a piece of string.
    c) As short as possible but including all the main points from the essay.

11) Write down four things you should check for when you read through your essay at the end.

12) How do you correct a spelling mistake?

13) What would you do if you needed to change a whole sentence?

14) What would you do if you decided your whole essay was a bit wrong and there were only five minutes to go?

Three Steps for an Essay

So you've had a good look at the <u>play</u>. In this section we'll look at <u>four kinds</u> of exam question — writing <u>about</u> a character, <u>as</u> a character, about the <u>mood</u>, and as a <u>director</u>.

Three Steps to Exam Success

These three steps are a <u>little treasure</u> for answering exam questions. And they work for <u>any kind</u> of Shakespeare question — bargain.

1) Read the question and underline the important bits.

2) Go through the set scenes and look for examples you could use in your answer.

3) Do a quick plan for your essay. Look back at this when you're writing so you don't run out of ideas.

See Section 5 for more about planning.

Writing About a Character

e.g. **Act 1 Scene 3 and Act 3 Scene 7**
In these scenes we learn about Richard's character.
How is Richard shown to be a dishonest character?
Support your ideas by referring to the scenes.

"Writing about", not "riding around".

Can't hear you.

1) Start by <u>underlining</u> the most <u>important</u> words in the question — you can write on the exam paper.

<u>How</u> is Richard shown to be a <u>dishonest</u> character?

You have to explain how Shakespeare lets the audience know Richard's a trickster.

The underlined words are the most important ones. They tell you what to write about.

2) Once you've got the question in your head, go through the scenes and <u>pick out sections</u> that look like they'll help your answer.

And thus I clothe my naked villainy
With odd old ends stol'n forth of holy writ,
And seem a saint when most I play the devil.
Act 1, Scene 3, 335-337

3) Go through the scenes again and check for things you <u>might have missed</u> — it looks really good if you can find points that are <u>relevant</u> but <u>not obvious</u>.

Steps? I thought they'd split up...

These questions shouldn't ask you anything <u>unexpected</u> — you should know about the characters and their odd little ways before the exam. Try and be really <u>thorough</u> and there'll be no hiccups.

Characters — The Bigger Picture

If you're asked to write about a <u>character</u> there are <u>a few things</u> you can do to get <u>more marks</u> — it's that thing about looking for the <u>less obvious stuff</u> again.

Some Characters are Complicated

1) Shakespeare's characters aren't always everything that they <u>seem</u> — if they were, they'd be pretty boring. Take Richard — he's constantly <u>pretending</u> to be something he's not, and he's <u>very good</u> at it.

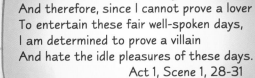

And therefore, since I cannot prove a lover
To entertain these fair well-spoken days,
I am determined to prove a villain
And hate the idle pleasures of these days.
Act 1, Scene 1, 28-31

2) The audience, know what he's doing, because he says at the start that he's <u>up to no good</u>.

3) Keep in mind what characters are trying to <u>achieve</u>, e.g. Richard really wants to become King, and he's prepared to <u>lie</u> and <u>kill</u> in order to achieve his goal.

It's a fair cop.

4) Some characters are <u>mostly bad</u> but have a few <u>good qualities</u>, e.g. Buckingham <u>accepts his fate</u> when he comes to have his head chopped off.

Remember Who's In Favour and Who's Not

People fall <u>in and out of Richard's favour</u> throughout the play. It's important to remember whether the character you're writing about is on Richard's side or against him, as this will <u>affect the character's behaviour</u>.

1) Hastings thinks Richard <u>likes</u> him, but then Richard goes and has him <u>executed</u>.

2) Richard goes out of his way to get Anne as his Queen, then has her <u>killed</u> when he decides he wants to <u>marry his niece</u> instead. Men eh?

3) Buckingham is Richard's <u>right-hand man</u> for a long time. He's <u>loyal</u> to Richard and helps him to <u>become King</u>. But even Buckingham ends up <u>running for his life</u> — unsuccessfully.

There are Loads of Characters in this Play

It's easy to think, "Oh my god, I'll <u>never remember</u> who all these people are". It's true that there are <u>lots</u> of characters, but the more you study the play, the more they all <u>fit into place</u>.

This is why it's dead important that you know what happens in the <u>whole play</u> — if you only read the set scenes, you won't know <u>who's who</u> or what they're <u>up to</u>.

Have a good look at pages 9-16 for more details on the characters.
Read pages 21-29 for a summary of what happens in the whole play.

That Richard, eh? What a character...

So that's one type of exam question. Writing <u>about</u> characters is probably the <u>simplest</u> of the four kinds of question we'll look at. On the next few pages we'll look at writing <u>as</u> a character.

Writing as a Character is HARD

The second type of question asks you to write as if <u>you are</u> a character in the play. This can be <u>tricky</u> — not only do you have to use your <u>imagination</u>, you've got to be <u>accurate</u> too.

You've Got to Really Know Your Stuff

Who are you meant to be?

Cliff.

For these questions, you've got to <u>pretend you're the character</u> you're writing about. You've also got to show you know the <u>whole play</u>, not just the set scenes. Don't panic though. Remember the <u>three steps</u> to writing an essay (page 36) — you can use them here too.

You Don't have to Pretend to be Shakespeare

1) Using the same <u>words</u> and <u>style of language</u> that Bill used would be more than a mite <u>difficult</u>. Good job you <u>don't have to do it</u>, then.

2) But you <u>do</u> have to use words that sound <u>right for the characters</u>. So if you're writing as <u>Buckingham</u>, you <u>shouldn't</u> write something like this:

> *Oo-er, it's getting a bit dodgy now... sounds like Richard's gonna chop my bonce off like the rest if I don't get on my bike pronto.*

It's <u>not accurate</u> — it doesn't sound like something Buckingham would say.

PLAYWRIGHTS IN THEIR EYES

Tonight, Matthew, I'm going to be...

3) It's a good idea to use <u>words or short quotes from the scenes</u> in your sentences. It shows you're clued up about the play.

Here's an Example

> **Act 4, Scene 2**
> Imagine you are Buckingham.
> Write down your thoughts and feelings after talking with Richard at the end of this scene.

Use 'I', 'we' and 'my' to show you're the character.

Work a brief quote into the answer.

> *I fear the worst now that Richard seems to mistrust me. <u>I've always been so loyal to him</u> — but <u>he's never hesitated to have people killed after falling out with them in the past.</u> When I <u>think on Hastings</u>, it appears the same thing could now happen to <u>me</u>.*
>
> *I must get away from him before it's too late.*

Show you know about the character.

Show you know the rest of the play.

Bill Shakes-beer — the nervous pub landlord...

Don't fall into the trap of using <u>he</u> or <u>she</u> — in this type of question, you <u>are</u> the character. Also, you need to make absolutely sure that what you say <u>matches</u> what happens in the play.

WRITING AS A
CHARACTER

Quotes and Reactions

Right, here's some more stuff about writing as a character. As I said on the last page, quotes can look really impressive in these questions. Here's how to make the most of them.

Keep the Quotes Short

Quoting in these questions is a bit different from slipping them in to a standard essay. It's very hard to make long quotes fit in naturally to what you're writing. The trick is to keep quotes short.

1) You can use words your character says in the play.

 It seems that Richard is angry because I asked for some pause to consider what he was asking of me. When he refused to repay my deep service by keeping his promise for the earldom, I thought about what had happened to people like Hastings.

 Hmm, now let me think...

These quotes sound right because they're short and fit in with what Buckingham says. You don't need to use speech marks if you do this — the examiner will know they're from the play.

2) You can quote other characters, not just the one you're writing as. This shows you're thinking about what just happened.

e.g. When Richard told me he was "not in the vein" to repay me, I realised that I had fallen out of his favour.

Say what Effect the Quote has on you

1) When you quote something your character said, you need to expand on it — explain the importance of it.

e.g. I have been of deep service to Richard for some time — in fact, I've been his most loyal follower. All I wanted was my just reward. Now it seems that this means nothing to him.

2) When you quote something someone else said, say how it made you feel.

e.g. When he told me he was "not in the vein" to repay me, I was amazed at his contempt for all I had done for him.

3) Make sure these comments on the quotes sound natural. Don't say things like "the reason I said that was...", or "my reaction to her saying that was..." — this sounds forced.

Status Quote — the studious rock band...

So the main points about quoting are: 1) Keep 'em short. 2) Show how your character reacts to the quotes. This'll make sure the quotes really add something to your answer.

How a Character Thinks and Feels

It's unbelievably important in these "pretend you're such and such" questions to really get into the character's <u>thoughts and feelings</u>.

Don't Just Tell the Story

The question <u>won't</u> ask what happens in a scene, it'll ask about its <u>effects</u>. So if you're asked to imagine you're a character, you'll need to write about <u>how you feel</u> and <u>what you think</u>.

 Act 1, Scene 2 and Act 4, Scene 1

Imagine you are Anne.

Write down your thoughts and feelings after discovering that Richard is not allowing visitors to see the young princes.

BAD ANSWER. D'OH!

> Queen Elizabeth, The Duchess of York and I were on our way to visit the princes. But then Brakenbury told us that we weren't allowed to see them. We pointed out that we were all related to the princes in some way, but Brakenbury still wouldn't let us see them. Then Stanley turned up and told me I had to go to Westminster to be crowned as Queen.

This is just <u>story-telling</u> — there's <u>no attempt</u> to understand how Anne <u>feels</u> at this point, which is what the question's about.

GOOD ANSWER. WOO-HOO!

This is miles better. It shows <u>briefly</u> that you know what <u>happened</u>, but focuses on how Anne <u>feels</u> — so it answers the question.

> I simply could not believe it when Brakenbury informed Queen Elizabeth, The Duchess of York and me that King Richard would not permit us to visit the gentle princes. We have every right to see them!
>
> I am now very fearful of becoming Richard's Queen. He seems to do as he pleases and doesn't feel the need to explain himself. I am afraid that he will shortly be rid of me, as this is clearly a sign that he cannot be trusted.

Use your Imagination

It's good to add your own <u>interpretation</u> when you're saying how a character feels — just make sure the <u>facts</u> still match what happens <u>in the play</u>.

> I now cannot believe I allowed myself to be wooed by the accursed Richard, after he killed my husband and father-in-law. I allowed my heart to be won over by his smooth words, and I should never have trusted him. I fear I may now pay the price for my rashness.

If you forget about him being a murderous hunchback, he's actually quite a catch....

How could you POSSIBLY know how I feel? (sob)

This kind of question is about being <u>imaginative</u> and <u>interesting</u>, but still using your <u>knowledge of the play</u>. Not easy, but get the <u>balance</u> right and Bob just may well be your dad's brother.

WRITING AS A CHARACTER | # What They Know and How They Speak

Here's a few more things to remember when writing <u>as a character</u>. I know I'm going on about this kind of question a lot, but there's loads of traps you can easily fall into.

You Know More than the Character does

When you see or read the whole play, you find out loads that the <u>characters don't know</u>. So watch out — if a character <u>isn't there</u> when something happens or someone says something, they <u>won't know</u> what happened or what's been said.

E.g. If you were writing as Clarence, you <u>wouldn't</u> say something like this:

> I don't believe Richard when he says he'll try and get me released. He said he's "determined to prove a villain", so I'm not going to trust him...

<u>DON'T SAY THIS</u> — Richard was <u>on his own</u> when he made that speech, so Clarence <u>didn't hear it</u>. In fact, Clarence is completely <u>taken in</u> by Richard's false promise.

You also need to remember the <u>order</u> things happen in — so if the question is about how a character feels in Act 3, <u>don't</u> mention stuff that happens in Act 4 or 5.

Think About How They'd Talk

1) Try to use <u>formal</u> language — most of the main characters in Richard III are quite <u>posh</u>.

2) It's usually best to <u>avoid slang</u> — the play is set <u>yonks ago</u>, so they don't often use the same words as we do today. If you use <u>insults</u>, there's plenty you can copy from the play, like "dog" and "foul devil".

3) Whichever character you're asked to be, you can use <u>brief quotes</u> from the play — this'll help you sound more <u>convincing</u> as the character you're writing as.

4) But you've got to use <u>your own words</u> too. It's really important that it's your own work and that you add <u>your own take</u> on it.

That Richard's bang out of order. I only wanted to pop in and check my kids were OK.

Richard's behaviour is very worrying. I fear for my children's safety.

How do they talk? They just open their mouths...

So there's <u>shed loads</u> to remember for these questions. But they do give you the opportunity to really go to town and show off your <u>understanding</u> of the characters. So it's worth it.

Questions About the Mood

Mood means the <u>feel</u> of a scene — whether it's tense, funny, exciting etc.

Mood *is Created in* Three Ways

1) <u>STAGE DIRECTIONS</u> — sometimes Shakespeare creates mood in the stage directions.

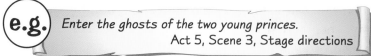

> *Enter the ghosts of the two young princes.*
> Act 5, Scene 3, Stage directions

Here the <u>ghosts</u> of the people Richard has murdered appear in his dreams, creating a spooky, <u>scary mood</u>.

2) <u>ANTICIPATION</u> — we want to know what will happen next. Shakespeare sometimes creates a feeling of suspense by letting the <u>audience</u> know something the <u>characters don't</u> — this is called <u>dramatic irony</u>.

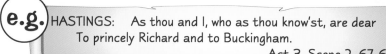

> HASTINGS: As thou and I, who as thou know'st, are dear
> To princely Richard and to Buckingham.
> Act 3, Scene 2, 67-68

What's going on?

Ant is a patient.

Here, Hastings tells Catesby that he's <u>mates with Richard</u>. But we, the audience, have heard Richard say that he'll <u>chop off Hastings' head</u> if he steps out of line — and sure enough, that's what happens.

3) <u>LANGUAGE</u> — this is Shakespeare's favourite method. E.g. The language Richard uses at the start of the play creates a dark, <u>sinister mood</u>:

I'm feeling a bit moo-dy...

Miserable cow.

> RICHARD: I am determined to prove a villain
> And hate the idle pleasures of these days.
> Act 1, Scene 1, 30-31

Richard admits right from the start that he has <u>no intention</u> of being <u>honourable</u>. Here he creates an <u>evil mood</u> that lasts for almost the entire play.

Mood *Questions Aren't as* Tricky *as They* Look

The thing is, the <u>wording</u> of these questions makes them look <u>really hard</u>. But you just need to <u>re-phrase</u> them and they're <u>much easier</u> to answer.

e.g.

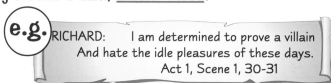

Explore how Shakespeare creates tension in Act 1, Scene 4.

This tells you that Act 1, Scene 4 is <u>tense</u>. "Explore" just means "<u>say</u>", or "<u>explain</u>". So the question becomes <u>much easier</u>.

Act 1, Scene 4 is <u>tense</u>. Say <u>how</u> Shakespeare <u>makes</u> it tense.

No atmosphere — like a Will Young concert...

Questions about mood <u>aren't</u> straightforward. But the set scenes you're tested on will have <u>plenty</u> of stuff to write about. And if you drop in stuff about <u>dramatic irony</u> it'll look well impressive.

WRITING ABOUT THE MOOD

How Mood Affects the Audience

When you answer a mood question, you need to really think about how the <u>audience</u> watching the play would be <u>feeling</u>.

How does Shakespeare _Make you Feel_ and _Why_?

If you're asked about the <u>mood of a scene</u>, talk about how it makes the audience <u>feel</u>.

(e.g.) _Act 1 Scene 3_
How does Shakespeare make the mood of this scene tense and hostile?

Tense and hostile...
How about some snakes? No...

Show you're answering the question.

Pick out what it is about certain words that make the audience feel certain things.

Shakespeare makes this scene tense and hostile through stage directions and his use of language. At first, Margaret lurks in the background, unseen by the other characters. She makes scathing aside comments about them, such as "Thou cacodemon!", referring to Richard. This makes the scene tense because we know that when she comes forward there will be trouble.

Margaret's language is full of bitter, violent feelings. For example, she calls the other characters "wrangling pirates", showing that she distrusts them and sees them as criminals fighting over her rightful position. Richard's response of "foul wrinkled witch" adds to the sense of hostility between the characters.

Explain your points — use "because".

Keep the answer focused and to-the-point.

Quote loads.

Show you _Understand Shakespeare_

To get top marks you have to show you <u>understand what's happening</u>, say how Shakespeare <u>affects the audience</u>, and give loads of <u>quotes</u>. Do all this and you're laughing.

Remember to write about:
1) Characters
2) Story
3) Language
4) Stage directions
5) The audience

I'm not in a mood — I'm revising...

Shakespeare <u>knew his audience</u> — the relationship between them <u>isn't complicated</u>.
If Shakey makes someone <u>fall over</u>, he's making the audience <u>laugh</u>. It's not rocket science.

Directing a Scene — The Audience

The <u>fourth</u> type of exam question you might get asks you to imagine you're a <u>director</u>.

Think About how the Play Should Look

The director's job is to put across his or her own <u>interpretation</u> of the play — so that the <u>audience</u> <u>understands</u> what's going on. Different directors have <u>different opinions</u> on things. Think about:

1) What <u>tone of voice</u> the actors should use, and how <u>loudly</u> or <u>softly</u> they should speak.

This director's a bit radical...

2) Where, how, and when the actors should <u>move</u> around the <u>stage</u> — e.g. whether they should <u>creep silently</u> around the edges or <u>stride boldly</u> onto centre stage.

3) Choosing the kind of <u>lighting</u>, <u>sound</u> and <u>set</u> the play needs to create the right <u>mood</u>.

4) Loads of other stuff, like the <u>clothes</u> and <u>make-up</u> the actors wear.

Use Loads of Quotes (again)

I've got it wrong again, haven't I?

Just like all the other types of question, you absolutely have to use <u>quotes</u> — but it's actually <u>dead easy</u> to stick a few quotes into these questions. <u>Follow these steps</u> and you're sorted:

- give your opinion about the mood or character
- find a quote that backs your idea up and write it down
- say how you want the actors to speak and act, and what lighting and sounds you'd use
- say why you'd do it (you won't get the marks otherwise)

e.g. Imagine you are a director.
How would you direct the murderers in Act 1 Scene 4?
Explain your ideas.

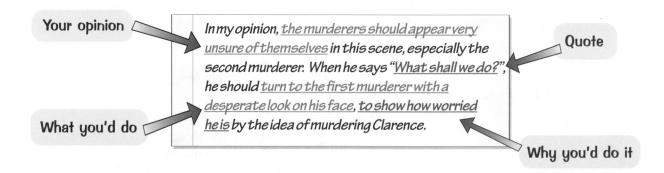

Your opinion

In my opinion, <u>the murderers should appear very unsure of themselves</u> in this scene, especially the second murderer. When he says "<u>What shall we do?</u>", he should <u>turn to the first murderer with a desperate look on his face</u>, <u>to show how worried he is</u> by the idea of murdering Clarence.

Quote

What you'd do

Why you'd do it

Die-rector — threatening a clergyman?

You should follow these steps in <u>every paragraph</u> (apart from the intro and the ending). This makes the whole thing a lot less painful and more <u>straightforward</u>. Sorted.

WRITING AS A DIRECTOR	# How the Characters Should Act

It's fair to say that the <u>most important</u> thing about Shakespeare is the <u>words</u> he uses. So as a director, you have to help the actors get the <u>meaning</u> of these words across to the <u>audience</u>.

How Should the Actors Say Their Lines?

1) Have a think about the <u>meaning</u> of the lines, then decide how you can <u>get this across</u> to the <u>audience</u>. It's all to do with <u>tone of voice</u> — e.g. angry, friendly, sarcastic.

2) <u>There's no right or wrong answer</u>. As long as you <u>explain why</u> you think an actor should speak in a certain way, and give some <u>evidence</u> from the play, you <u>can't go wrong</u>.

3) You can even suggest <u>more than one way</u> for the actor to speak a line — the examiner will like this, as it shows you're <u>thinking</u> really hard about the play. Just make sure you give <u>reasons</u> for each suggestion you make.

e.g. *In Act 2, Scene 1, when King Edward says "Is Clarence dead? The order was reversed", he is shocked by Richard's news. The actor could show this by <u>saying this line slowly and quietly, his voice shaking</u>.*

<u>On the other hand, he could shout this line, looking around him for someone to blame. This would show the anger and confusion caused by Richard's scheming.</u>

Give an idea about <u>how</u> the lines should be said.

Give <u>another opinion</u> if you have one.

Always <u>explain</u> why you have a certain idea. This is the <u>most important</u> part of your answer.

Think About how Different Characters will Act

<u>Different characters</u> will act in different ways. You can <u>compare</u> characters to show how <u>mood</u> is put across to the audience.

e.g. *Although King Edward is shocked, Richard knows exactly what is going on, and would sound calmer. However, he might also pretend to be sad about Clarence's death, and could say the line "But he, poor man, by your first order died", in a reflective, regretful tone.*

Show that you know they <u>don't all feel the same</u>.

Here's your <u>explanation</u> again — really important.

Think about how the characters are <u>feeling</u>, then how to <u>show this</u> in their <u>tone of voice</u>. And remember you can <u>compare</u> different characters and their <u>feelings</u> in the same scene.

<u>Linking words</u> are dead useful. They help you move from one part of your answer to the next.

- however
- although
- on the other hand
- in comparison

Shtop! Thish play is not ready yet...

Being a director means giving your own <u>interpretation</u> of the play. You can watch versions of the play on video for <u>ideas</u> — but make sure you add your own <u>slant</u>. And be <u>enthusiastic</u> — it works.

Appearance & What Characters Do

As I said earlier, directors have loads of <u>other stuff</u> to scratch their heads about as well as how the actors should say their lines. You need to <u>mention these</u> when you answer the question.

Tell the Actors How to Move

They're actors, so make 'em <u>act</u>. Their <u>body language</u> has a big effect on how their characters come across, and you can suggest things that aren't in the stage directions. As ever, you've got to <u>explain your ideas</u> and stick to the <u>evidence</u> in the play.

 e.g. *In Act 1, Scene 3, the actor playing Margaret should at first crouch near the back of the stage, to show she is hiding from the other characters. Then, when she comes forward, she should stride boldly into the middle of the stage. In my opinion, when she says "But repetition of what thou hast marred", she should turn violently towards Richard and stab her finger in his chest, to show her hatred and aggression towards him.*

Use phrases like "<u>in my opinion</u>" — they show it's <u>your idea</u> and you're <u>exploring</u> the play, rather than jumping to one conclusion and sticking to it.

Mention What Sound and Lighting You'd Use

1) <u>Sound</u> can be used to create a <u>mood</u>. In Act 2, Scene 1, when Richard announces that Clarence is dead, it could go from being <u>quiet</u> and <u>peaceful</u> to having a lot of <u>background noise</u> and <u>exclamations</u> from the other characters — the stage direction, *"They all start"*, suggests this.

I said "lighting" not "lightning".

DIRECTOR

2) <u>Lighting</u> is also pretty crucial. There are often <u>clues</u> in the text for what kind of lighting you could use, e.g. In Act 5, Scene 3, Richard says "The sun will not be seen to-day", so the lighting could be fairly <u>dim</u>, to create the impression of an overcast day.

3) Remember to <u>explain</u> every suggestion you make. I know I sound like a broken record saying this, but you <u>absolutely, positively, definitely</u> have to do this. Honestly. I really, really mean it.

Say What Clothes They Should Wear

You can show you understand a scene by talking about the <u>costumes</u> you'd choose for it.

 e.g. *When Richmond delivers his oration to his soldiers in Act 5, Scene 3, he should be dressed in full armour to show that he is leading his troops into battle, holding his helmet at his side ready for the start of the fight.*

You <u>don't</u> have to stick to <u>old-fashioned</u> costumes. Lots of productions today use <u>modern clothes</u> and you can too — as long as you can show how they <u>suit the characters</u>.

Background music? Sound idea...

Shakespeare was a bit <u>vague</u> about things like body language and lighting — so there's loads of scope for using your <u>imagination</u>. Just make sure you <u>back your ideas up</u> with quotes and stuff.

WRITING AS A DIRECTOR	# Directing — The Mood

The director can also create <u>mood</u> for the <u>audience</u> by thinking about how to get the actors to say their <u>words</u> with a bit of feeling.

Words can Create a Mood

1) There are loads of opportunities for a director to play around with Shakespeare's <u>words</u> to create different <u>moods</u>.

2) If Anne spoke in a <u>happy</u>, <u>relieved</u> way here, it would suggest that she has been completely <u>taken in</u> by Richard. But she could say these lines in a more <u>hesitant</u>, <u>uncertain</u> manner, suggesting that she's still got her <u>doubts</u> about Richard.

> **e.g.** ANNE: With all my heart, and much it joys me too,
> To see you are become so penitent.
> Act 1, Scene 2, 219-220

3) As a director, you need to decide what kind of <u>mood</u> fits in with the <u>characters</u> on the stage in that scene — then think about how to <u>create</u> that mood.

> Well, a girl can change her mind, can't she?

4) Your knowledge of the <u>whole play</u> is vital — we know Richard's a <u>baddie</u>, so the mood when he's on stage should usually be <u>dark</u> and <u>threatening</u>.

Watch Out for Mood Changes Within Scenes

The <u>mood</u> in a scene often <u>changes</u> quite quickly. The <u>audience</u> should <u>feel</u> this — it's what keeps them <u>interested</u> in the play. You can show the change in mood through changes in a particular character's <u>tone of voice</u>.

> **e.g.** The mood of Act 2, Scene 1 changes when Richard announces that Clarence is dead. When King Edward says "A pleasing cordial", he should sound satisfied and relieved, creating a <u>relaxed and happy mood</u>.
>
> However, Richard's news puts an end to this peaceful feel. At the end of the scene, <u>King Edward bitterly regrets the death of Clarence</u>. When he asks who "Kneeled at my feet and bid me be advised?", he should sound <u>very regretful and angry, making the tone much darker</u> than at the start of the scene.

Show you understand how the characters feel.

Explain what sort of mood you are trying to create and how.

Say how you would create the mood you want.

Heaven knows I'm miserable now... but not now...

So there's <u>a lot to think about</u> in these what-if-you-were-the-director style questions. But they're a really good opportunity to give a good "<u>discussion</u>" — and the <u>more ideas</u> you have, the <u>better</u>.

Revision Summary

So there you have it. Four types of exam question, and oodles of tips to help you with each one. Fair enough, some are easier than others — but you've gotta be well prepared for <u>any</u> of those types of question, 'cos you just don't know what'll come up in the exam. And if the sight of the very word "exam" has you breaking out in a cold sweat, it's time to really get learning. Right, enough from me, let's have a butcher's at how much attention you've been paying in this section...

1) Name three useful things you should do before you start writing an answer to an exam question.

2) What's the best way to work out who all the characters are?
   a) Read the whole play. b) Just read the set scenes.   c) Do loads of historical research.

3) Should you pretend to be Shakespeare when you're writing as a character?

4) When writing as a character, should the quotes you use be long or short?

5) What should you *always* do after quoting?

   a) Stand up and say the quote out loud.

   b) Explain why the quote is relevant to what you're writing.

   c) Talk about the mood.

6) Is it good or bad to use your imagination when you're writing as a character?

7) Why is the order things happen in the play important when writing as a character?

8) What kind of language do most of the characters in *Richard III* use?

   a) Slang   b) Formal language   c) Welsh

9) What does "mood" mean?

10) Name three ways Shakespeare creates mood.

11) What is "dramatic irony"?

12) What should you do to make mood questions easier to answer?

   a) Re-phrase the question.   b) Ignore the bits you don't understand.   c) Cheer up a bit.

13) When you answer questions about mood, you should think about Shakespeare's effect on:

   a) the director   b) the audience   c) post-war politics

14) Name four things you could write about if you're writing as the director.

15) Should the clothes you make the actor wear always be old-fashioned?

16) How could you show the change in mood within a scene?

17) What do you absolutely, positively have to do every time you make a point in an essay?

   a) Explain the point and give evidence. b) Say what lighting you'd use. c) Play a fanfare.

The set scenes are the only scenes you need to know in real detail.
Make sure you know these two scenes inside out.

This is the very start of the play. England is at peace after a war between the House of York and the House of Lancaster. Edward IV, a Yorkist, is now on the throne. His younger brother Richard is ambitious to have more power and decides to cause some trouble...

ACT 1 SCENE 1

Outside the Tower of London.
Enter RICHARD, DUKE OF GLOUCESTER.

1-8 "We're finally at peace now Edward's on the throne. Instead of fighting, we can all have a good time." →	RICHARD Now is the winter of our discontent
	Made glorious summer by this son of York,
son of York = *Edward IV*	And all the clouds that loured upon our house
loured = *scowled*	In the deep bosom of the ocean buried.
bruised arms = *damaged weapons*	Now are our brows bound with victorious wreaths, 5
	Our bruised arms hung up for monuments,
alarums = *calls to arms*	Our stern alarums changed to merry meetings,
measures = *dances*	Our dreadful marches to delightful measures.
	Grim-visaged war hath smoothed his wrinkled front,
9-12 Richard implies that now the war's over, Edward IV is having a love affair. →	And now, instead of mounting barbed steeds 10
	To fright the souls of fearful adversaries,
front = *forehead*	He capers nimbly in a lady's chamber
	To the lascivious pleasing of a lute.
14-17 Richard says that he's too ugly to have a love affair. →	But I, that am not shaped for sportive tricks,
	Nor made to court an amorous looking-glass, 15
rudely stamped = *ugly*	I, that am rudely stamped, and want love's majesty
want = *lack*	To strut before a wanton ambling nymph,
nymph = *a pretty lady*	I, that am curtailed of this fair proportion,
curtailed = *denied*	Cheated of feature by dissembling Nature,
	Deformed, unfinished, sent before my time 20
22-23 "I look so bad that dogs bark at me if I stand near them." →	Into this breathing world, scarce half made up,
	And that so lamely and unfashionable
	That dogs bark at me as I halt by them;
24-25 Richard says that he finds peace-time pretty boring. →	Why, I, in this weak piping time of peace,
	Have no delight to pass away the time, 25
	Unless to spy my shadow in the sun
descant = *talk about*	And descant on mine own deformity.
	And therefore, since I cannot prove a lover
28-30 "If I can't have a good time having an affair, then I'll have a good time being a villain and causing trouble." →	To entertain these fair well-spoken days,
	I am determined to prove a villain 30
	And hate the idle pleasures of these days.
inductions = *preparations*	Plots have I laid, inductions dangerous,
libels = *false claims*	By drunken prophecies, libels, and dreams,
	To set my brother Clarence and the King
32-35 Richard says he's plotted to set his two brothers (King Edward IV and the Duke of Clarence) against one another. →	In deadly hate the one against the other. 35

And if King Edward be as true and just
As I am subtle, false, and treacherous,
This day should Clarence closely be mewed up,
About a prophecy, which says that 'G'
Of Edward's heirs the murderer shall be.   40
Dive, thoughts, down to my soul: here Clarence comes.

      Enter CLARENCE, BRAKENBURY *and guards.*

Brother, good day; what means this armed guard
That waits upon your grace?

CLARENCE   His Majesty,
Tend'ring my person's safety, hath appointed
This conduct to convey me to the Tower.   45

RICHARD Upon what cause?

CLARENCE   Because my name is George.

RICHARD Alack, my lord, that fault is none of yours.
He should, for that, commit your godfathers.
O, belike his Majesty hath some intent
That you should be new-christened in the Tower.   50
But what's the matter, Clarence? May I know?

CLARENCE Yea, Richard, when I know: for I protest
As yet I do not. But, as I can learn,
He hearkens after prophecies and dreams,
And from the cross-row plucks the letter G,   55
And says a wizard told him that by G
His issue disinherited should be.
And, for my name of George begins with G,
It follows in his thought that I am he.
These, as I learn, and such like toys as these   60
Have moved his highness to commit me now.

RICHARD Why, this it is, when men are ruled by women.
'Tis not the King that sends you to the Tower:
My Lady Grey his wife, Clarence, 'tis she
That tempers him to this extremity.   65
Was it not she and that good man of worship,
Anthony Woodville, her brother there,
That made him send Lord Hastings to the Tower,
From whence this present day he is delivered?
We are not safe, Clarence, we are not safe.   70

mewed up = *imprisoned*

38-40 "Hopefully Clarence will be locked up today, because of that prophecy which says someone called 'G' will murder Edward IV's heirs." Richard has encouraged Edward IV to think 'G' means Clarence because Clarence's first name is George. Actually, 'G' means Richard, as he's the Duke of Gloucester.

43-45 Clarence says he is being sent to the Tower of London by Edward IV.

conduct = *guard*

46 Richard pretends he doesn't know why Clarence is being imprisoned.

Being two-faced has never been a problem for me.

belike = *perhaps*

51 Richard keeps up the pretence of not knowing what's going on.

hearkens = *listens*

cross-row = *alphabet*

issue = *children*

toys = *fancies, trifles*

commit = *imprison*

63-65 Richard stirs things up further by blaming Edward IV's wife Elizabeth for Clarence being locked up. He claims that Elizabeth was also responsible for a nobleman called Hastings being imprisoned.

Lady Grey = *Elizabeth Woodville, Edward IV's wife*

delivered = *set free*

70 Richard sympathises with Clarence and pretends he's on his side. The lying little toe-rag...

Be afraid of 'G'. 'G' will kill your children, disinherit you, drag your kingdom into the fiery furnace...

All I wanted was some racing tips.

CLARENCE By heaven, I think there is no man secure
But the Queen's kindred and night-walking heralds
That trudge betwixt the King and Mistress Shore.
Heard you not what an humble suppliant
Lord Hastings was to her for his delivery? 75

RICHARD Humbly complaining to her deity
Got my Lord Chamberlain his liberty.
I'll tell you what, I think it is our way,
If we will keep in favour with the King,
To be her men and wear her livery. 80
The jealous o'er-worn widow and herself,
Since that our brother dubbed them gentlewomen,
Are mighty gossips in our monarchy.

BRAKENBURY I beseech your graces both to pardon me;
His Majesty hath straitly given in charge 85
That no man shall have private conference,
Of what degree soever, with his brother.

RICHARD Even so? An please your worship, Brakenbury,
You may partake of any thing we say.
We speak no treason, man: we say the King 90
Is wise and virtuous, and his noble Queen
Well struck in years, fair, and not jealous.
We say that Shore's wife hath a pretty foot,
A cherry lip, a bonny eye, a passing pleasing tongue,
And that the Queen's kindred are made gentlefolks. 95
How say you sir? Can you deny all this?

BRAKENBURY With this, my lord, myself have nought to do.

RICHARD Naught to do with mistress Shore! I tell thee, fellow,
He that doth naught with her (excepting one)
Were best to do it secretly, alone. 100

BRAKENBURY What one, my lord?

RICHARD Her husband, knave. Wouldst thou betray me?

BRAKENBURY I beseech your grace to pardon me, and withal
Forbear your conference with the noble Duke.

CLARENCE We know thy charge, Brakenbury, and will obey. 105

RICHARD We are the Queen's abjects, and must obey.
Brother, farewell. I will unto the King,
And whatsoever you will employ me in,
Were it to call King Edward's widow "sister",
I will perform it to enfranchise you. 110

52

Meantime, this deep disgrace in brotherhood
Touches me deeper than you can imagine.

CLARENCE   I know it pleaseth neither of us well.

RICHARD   Well, your imprisonment shall not be long.
I will deliver you or else lie for you.   115
Meantime, have patience.

CLARENCE   I must perforce. Farewell.
Exeunt CLARENCE, BRAKENBURY *and guards.*

RICHARD   Go, tread the path that thou shalt ne'er return.
Simple, plain Clarence! I do love thee so,
That I will shortly send thy soul to heaven,
If heaven will take the present at our hands.   120
But who comes here? The new-delivered Hastings?

111-112 On the surface this sounds like a nice thing to say. But there's a double-meaning in it — Richard has betrayed Clarence, and Clarence doesn't know it yet.

114 This could mean that Clarence will be released soon. Or it could mean that he'll be dead soon...

115 Another double-meaning — "lie for you" could mean "take your place" or it could mean "tell lies about you".

perforce = *unavoidably*

ne'er = *never*

118-119 Clarence has left the stage now, and Richard talks openly about his plans to have him killed.

Er, Richard... Did you just say something about killing me?

It was a soliloquy, Clarence. You were off stage. Forget about it, will ya?

In this scene, Buckingham and Richard try to persuade the Mayor that Richard should be King. They do a sort of double-act: Buckingham praises Richard, and Richard acts all humble and modest. By the end of the scene, they've won the Mayor over, and Richard is all set to be the new King of England.

ACT 3 SCENE 7

Enter RICHARD *aloft, between two Bishops.*

MAYOR   See, where his grace stands between two clergymen!   95

BUCKINGHAM   Two props of virtue for a Christian prince,
To stay him from the fall of vanity:
And, see, a book of prayer in his hand,
True ornaments to know a holy man.
Famous Plantagenet, most gracious prince,   100
Lend favourable ear to our requests;
And pardon us the interruption
Of thy devotion and right Christian zeal.

RICHARD   My lord, there needs no such apology:
I do beseech your Grace to pardon me,   105
Who, earnest in the service of my God,
Deferred the visitation of my friends.
But, leaving this, what is your grace's pleasure?

BUCKINGHAM   Even that, I hope, which pleaseth God above,
And all good men of this ungoverned isle.   110

RICHARD   I do suspect I have done some offence
That seems disgracious in the city's eye,
And that you come to reprehend my ignorance.

BUCKINGHAM   You have, my lord. Would it might please your grace,
On our entreaties, to amend your fault!   115

RICHARD   Else wherefore breathe I in a Christian land?

BUCKINGHAM   Know then, it is your fault that you resign
The supreme seat, the throne majestical,
The sceptred office of your ancestors,
Your state of fortune and your due of birth,   120
The lineal glory of your royal house,
To the corruption of a blemished stock:
Whiles, in the mildness of your sleepy thoughts,
Which here we waken to our country's good,
The noble isle doth want her proper limbs;   125
Her face defaced with scars of infamy,
Her royal stock graft with ignoble plants,
And almost shouldered in the swallowing gulf
Of dark forgetfulness and deep oblivion.

Two props of virtue = the two bishops

stay = stop

96-99 Buckingham emphasises how religious Richard is. This is part of their strategy for impressing the Mayor.

Plantagenet = a line of English Kings which Richard is descended from.

Lend favourable ears = listen sympathetically

zeal = enthusiasm

110 Buckingham's hinting at the fact that England needs a new ruler now Edward IV has died.

111 "Oh dear, have I done something wrong?"

reprehend = tell off

entreaties = requests

wherefore = why

117-118 "Yes, you have done something wrong — you've refused to become King."

sceptred office = role of King

122 Earlier in the play, Richard and Buckingham spread rumours that Edward IV's kids were illegitimate. This is what Buckingham means by "blemished stock".

127 "The royal blood has been mixed with that of unworthy people. The Royal House might be lost and forgotten forever."

I love a good metaphor.

Which to recure, we heartily solicit 130
Your gracious self to take on you the charge
And kingly government of this your land,
Not as protector, steward, substitute,
Or lowly factor for another's gain; 135
But as successively from blood to blood,
Your right of birth, your empery, your own.
For this, consorted with the citizens,
Your very worshipful and loving friends,
And by their vehement instigation, 140
In this just cause come I to move your grace.

RICHARD   I cannot tell if to depart in silence,
Or bitterly to speak in your reproof,
Best fitteth my degree or your condition.
If not to answer, you might haply think
Tongue-tied ambition, not replying, yielded 145
To bear the golden yoke of sovereignty,
Which fondly you would here impose on me.
If to reprove you for this suit of yours,
So seasoned with your faithful love to me,
Then, on the other side, I checked my friends. 150
Therefore, to speak, and to avoid the first,
And then, in speaking, not to incur the last,
Definitively thus I answer you.
Your love deserves my thanks, but my desert
Unmeritable shuns your high request. 155
First, if all obstacles were cut away,
And that my path were even to the crown,
As my ripe revenue and due of birth
Yet so much is my poverty of spirit,
So mighty and so many my defects, 160
That I would rather hide me from my greatness,
Being a bark to brook no mighty sea,
Than in my greatness covet to be hid,
And in the vapour of my glory smothered.
But, God be thanked, there is no need of me, 165
And much I need to help you, were there need;
The royal tree hath left us royal fruit,
Which, mellowed by the stealing hours of time,
Will well become the seat of majesty,
And make, no doubt, us happy by his reign. 170
On him I lay that you would lay on me,
The right and fortune of his happy stars,
Which God defend that I should wring from him!

recure = restore to health

130-132 "We want you to be King."

133-136 Richard's not technically the heir to the throne — Prince Edward is. Buckingham's telling Richard not to be Prince Edward's adviser, but to take the crown himself, instead.

empery = empire

137-140 Buckingham says that the citizens really like Richard and want him to be King. (This is a fib.)

move = persuade

speak in your reproof = say that you're wrong

141-150 Richard says he doesn't know whether to speak or not — if he stays silent they might think he wants the crown. But if he tells them he doesn't want it, they might be offended.

fondly = foolishly

checked = rebuked

154-155 "I don't deserve the crown." Remember Richard's playing hard to get — he does want the crown really.

159-160 Richard sounds really modest here, but it's just part of the act he's putting on.

bark = ship

This old thing? It's nothing special....

covet = wants

167-169 "Prince Edward will make a good King when he's a bit older."

172-173 "I couldn't take Prince Edward's place!"

I'm a love man.

nice and trivial = *unimportant*

177-178 "Prince Edward is illegitimate."

contract = *engaged*

183-185 "Edward IV broke his previous engagement so that he could marry Elizabeth." Buckingham is really rude about Elizabeth — he says she's old, ugly, unhappy...

base declension = *loss of standards*

bigamy = *being married to more than one person.*

191 "We only call Edward a prince out of politeness."

expostulate = *argue*

195-196 "Take the Crown."

198-200 "You will restore the honour of the House of York, after Edward and Elizabeth brought shame on it."

201 "Yes, take the crown — we all think you should."

suit = *appeal, request*

206-207 "I'm sorry, but I couldn't possibly become King."

208-215 "You might refuse the crown because you feel sorry for Prince Edward. But you should remember that because Prince Edward is illegitimate, he's never going to become King."

effeminate remorse = *tender pity*

all estates = *people of all social classes*

BUCKINGHAM   My lord, this argues conscience in your grace,
But the respects thereof are nice and trivial,   175
All circumstances well considered.
You say that Edward is your brother's son:
So say we too, but not by Edward's wife,
For first he was contract to Lady Lucy—
Your mother lives a witness to that vow—   180
And afterward by substitute betrothed
To Bona, sister to the King of France.
These both put off, a poor petitioner,
A care-crazed mother to a many sons,
A beauty-waning and distressed widow,   185
Even in the afternoon of her best days,
Made prize and purchase of his wanton eye,
Seduced the pitch and height of his degree
To base declension and loathed bigamy.
By her, in his unlawful bed, he got   190
This Edward, whom our manners call the prince.
More bitterly could I expostulate,
Save that, for reverence to some alive,
I give a sparing limit to my tongue.
Then, good my lord, take to your royal self   195
This proffered benefit of dignity;
If not to bless us and the land withal,
Yet to draw forth your noble ancestry
From the corruption of abusing times,
Unto a lineal true-derived course.   200

MAYOR   Do, good my lord, your citizens entreat you.

BUCKINGHAM   Refuse not, mighty lord, this proffered love.

CATESBY   O, make them joyful, grant their lawful suit!

RICHARD   Alas, why would you heap this care on me?
I am unfit for state and majesty.   205
I do beseech you, take it not amiss,
I cannot nor I will not yield to you.

BUCKINGHAM   If you refuse it — as, in love and zeal,
Loath to depose the child, your brother's son;
As well we know your tenderness of heart   210
And gentle, kind, effeminate remorse,
Which we have noted in you to your kindred,
And equally indeed to all estates—
Yet know, whether you accept our suit or no,
Your brother's son shall never reign our king,   215

Section 7 — The Set Scenes

> But we will plant some other in the throne,
> To the disgrace and downfall of your house,
> And in this resolution here we leave you.
> Come, citizens. 'Zounds! I'll entreat no more.

RICHARD   O, do not swear, my lord of Buckingham.   220

Exit BUCKINGHAM, MAYOR and Citizens.

CATESBY   Call him again, sweet prince, and accept their suit.
> If you deny them, all the land will rue it.

RICHARD   Will you enforce me to a world of cares?
> Call them again. I am not made of stones,
> But penetrable to your kind entreaties,   225
> Albeit against my conscience and my soul.

Enter BUCKINGHAM and the rest.

> Cousin of Buckingham, and sage, grave men,
> Since you will buckle fortune on my back,
> To bear her burden, whe'er I will or no,
> I must have patience to endure the load.   230
> But if black scandal or foul-faced reproach
> Attend the sequel of your imposition,
> Your mere enforcement shall acquittance me
> From all the impure blots and stains thereof;
> For God doth know, and you may partly see,   235
> How far I am from the desire of this.

MAYOR   God bless your grace! We see it, and will say it.

RICHARD   In saying so, you shall but say the truth.

BUCKINGHAM   Then I salute you with this royal title:
> Long live King Richard, England's worthy King!   240

ALL   Amen.

BUCKINGHAM   Tomorrow may it please you to be crowned?

RICHARD   Even when you please, for you will have it so.

BUCKINGHAM   Tomorrow, then, we will attend your grace,
> And so most joyfully we take our leave.   245

RICHARD   Come, let us to our holy work again.
> Farewell my cousin, farewell gentle friends.

Exeunt.

216-217 *"If you don't take the crown, we'll give it to someone else and it'll be the downfall of the House of York."*

Naughty boy, Bucks.

'Zounds! = *My God!*

entreat = *say, plead*

rue = *regret*

224-226 *"You've persuaded me. It's against my better judgement, but I'll accept the crown."*

whe'er = *whether*

231-234 *"I can't be blamed if anything goes wrong when I'm King, because I didn't want to do it in the first place."*

imposition = *the burden of kingship*

acquittance = *acquit, excuse*

242-243 *Richard's finally got what he wants — he's going to be crowned King of England. He stays cool though, still pretending that he's only doing it because they've asked him.*

Index

58

Index